Practicing Running Time Analysis of Recursive Algorithms

Irena Pevac

ISBN: 1539088863
ISBN-13: 9781539088868

DEDICATION

This book is dedicated to the memory of Terezija, Tomislav, and Woody Bledsoe.

ACKNOWLEDGMENTS

The author is deeply grateful to professor Anany Levitin for taking the time to read the preliminary version of this book and to suggest several improvements. Thanks also to student Paulo Nunes for his diligent work to proofread the text. Finally, thanks to Central Connecticut State University for granting me the sabbatical leave which enabled the completion of this project.

PREFACE

The book contains practice examples of time performance analysis of various types of recursive algorithms. It is intended to supplement textbooks of Algorithms and/or Data Structures courses for topics devoted to time performance analysis of recursive algorithms. Over 50 examples of decrease-by-constant, decrease-by-constant-factor, divide-and-conquer, and general-decrease type covered in chapters 1 through 4 should help learners to become proficient in time efficiency analysis. Practice problems are provided with specification of the problem description in English, implementation in Java, and complete time analysis which includes specifying problem size, specifying basic operation, and recurrences, and at the end we provide detailed derivation of the solution for recurrence.

Chapter 1 Running Time Analysis of Decrease-by-Constant Type Recursive Algorithms

The first chapter contains recursive algorithms of size n that invoke one sub-problem of size n reduced by a positive integer constant c. The corresponding recurrences are of type $T(n) = T(n - c) + f(n)$. Function $f(n)$ denotes the cost of the non-recursive portion of the code.

Chapter 2 Running Time Analysis of Decrease-by-Constant-Factor Recursive Algorithms

The second chapter contains recursive algorithms of size n that invoke one sub-problem of size n reduced by a constant factor b, where b is a positive integer that does not depend on n. The corresponding recurrences are of type $T(n) = T(n / b) + f(n)$. Function $f(n)$ denotes the cost of the non-recursive portion of the code.

Chapter 3 Running Time Analysis of Divide-and-Conquer Type Recursive Algorithms

The third chapter contains recursive algorithms of size n that invoke a subproblem with problem size reduced by positive constant factor b ($b > 1$). Parameter a is a positive integer constant. The recurrences are of type $T(n) = a\,T(n / b) + f(n)$. Function $f(n)$ denotes the cost of the non-recursive portion of the code.

Chapter 4 Running Time Analysis of General-Decrease Type Recursive Algorithms

The fourth chapter contains recursive algorithms that are generalization of decrease-by-constant type. The problems discussed here are examples of size n characterized by second-order linear recurrence with constant coefficients of the form $a\,T(n) + b\,T(n-1) + c\,T(n-2) = f(n)$. Constants $a, b,$ and c are integer numbers, and a is not zero. We start with special cases when $a = 1$, $b = -2$, and $c = 0$ and $f(n) = 1$, followed by example when $a = 1$, $b = -1$, $c = -1$, and $f(n) = 1$. At the end we discuss recursive algorithms that invoke n subproblems of size reduced by one. This time the number of subproblems is no longer constant positive integer, but instead, is a linear function of n.

Chapter 5 Templates for Basic Time Performance Complexity Categories

We believe that students should recognize the following basic categories of algorithms: logarithmic, linear, $n \log n$, quadratic, polynomial, exponential, and n!. So, the fifth chapter provides an attempt to give characterization of common types of recurrences that result in specific running time performance. More precisely we provide a set of templates for the following seven basic time performance complexity categories: $\log n, n, n \log n, n^2, n^3, a^n$, and $n!$. The complexity category of some function $f(n)$ is the set of all functions that have the same asymptotic growth as $f(n)$, which is denoted $\Theta(f(n))$. The template examples are simple, and their time efficiency analysis is not mathematically intensive. If we replace basic operations with printing one letter, we can use such algorithms as representatives of the entire equivalence class of all performance equivalent algorithms. For each template we also specify which simple modifications do not affect its asymptotic performance. Finally, we list some algorithms that can be implemented by using the given template or its variation.

Irena Pevac
Central Connecticut State University

CONTENTS

CHAPTER 1

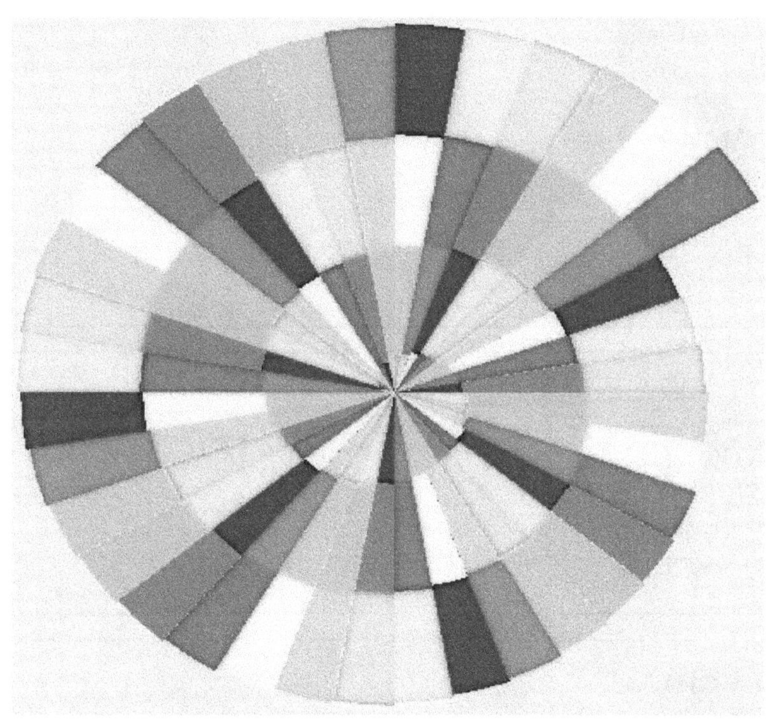

RUNNING TIME ANALYSIS OF DECREASE-BY-CONSTANT RECURSIVE ALGORITHMS

Recurrences type: T(n) = T(n-c) + f(n).
Constant c is positive integer and function f(n) is nonrecursive cost.

This chapter covers examples of time performance analysis of recursive algorithms of decrease-by-constant type. It includes problems of size n that invoke one sub-problem of size n reduced by a positive integer constant c. Each example contains a problem description, and a recursive algorithm implemented in Java followed by a full running time analysis. The analysis includes specifying problem size, basic operation, recurrences, and derivation of the solution for recurrences. The recurrences are of type T(n) = T(n - c) + f(n). Function f(n) denotes the cost of the nonrecursive portion of the code.

EXAMPLES

1) Algorithm determines factorial for nonnegative integer n.

```
//PRECONDITION: n≥0
int factorial(int n)
{
  if (n == 0)
    return 1;
  else
    return n * factorial(n-1);
}
```

ANALYSIS

BASIC OPERATION:	*
PROBLEM SIZE:	n
RECURRENCE BASE CASE:	T(0) = 0
RECURRENCE RECURSIVE STEP:	T(n) = T(n-1) + 1

SOLVING RECURRENCE

T(0) = 0
T(n) = T(n-1) + 1, for n>0.
    = (T(n-2) + 1) + 1
    = T(n-2) + 2
    = (T(n-3) + 1) + 2
    = T(n-3) + 3
    ...
    = T(n-n) + n
    = T(0) + n
    = n
T(n) is in Θ(n). T(n) is linear.

2) Algorithm computes d raised to the power of n, where n is a nonnegative integer and d is not equal to zero. The following definition is used to implement the code. If n is 0, $d^n = 1$. Otherwise, $d^n = d*d^{n-1}$.

```
//PRECONDITION n≥0, d≠0
public double power(double d, int n)
{
     if (n == 0)
        return 1.0;
     else
        return d * power(d, n - 1);
}
```

ANALYSIS

BASIC OPERATION:	*
PROBLEM SIZE:	n
RECURRENCE BASE CASE:	T(0) = 0
RECURRENCE RECURSIVE STEP:	T(n) = T(n-1) + 1

SOLVING RECURRENCE

T(0) = 0
T(n) = T(n-1) + 1, for n>0.
= T(n-2) + 2
= T(n-3) + 3
. . .
= T(n-n) + n
= T(0) + n
= n
T(n) is in Θ(n). T(n) is linear.

3) Algorithm computes the sum of the first n positive integers, 1 + 2 + 3 + … + n.

```
//PRECONDITION n>0
int sumFirstn(int n)
{
   if (n == 1)
      return 1;
```

```
  else
    return n + sumFirstn(n-1);
}
```

ANALYSIS

BASIC OPERATION:	+
PROBLEM SIZE:	n
RECURRENCE BASE CASE:	T(1) = 0
RECURRENCE RECURSIVE STEP:	T(n) = T(n-1) + 1

SOLVING RECURRENCE

T(1) = 0
T(n) = T(n-1) + 1, for n>1.
= T(n-2) + 2
= T(n-3) + 3
. . .
= T(n-(n-1)) + n-1
= T(1) + n-1
= n-1
T(n) is in Θ(n). T(n) is linear.

4) Given a positive integer value n, algorithm computes the sum of squares of the first n positive integers, $1^2 + 2^2 + 3^2 + ... + n^2$.

```
//PRECONDITION n>0
int sumSquares(int n)
{
  if (n == 1)
    return 1;
  else
    return n*n + sumSquares(n-1);
}
```

ANALYSIS	
BASIC OPERATION:	*
PROBLEM SIZE:	n

RECURRENCE BASE CASE:	T(1) = 0
RECURRENCE RECURSIVE STEP:	T(n) = T(n-1) + 1

SOLVING RECURRENCE

T(1) = 0
T(n) = T(n-1) + 1, for n>1.
= T(n-2) + 2
= T(n-3) + 3
. . .
= T(n-(n-1)) + n-1
= T(1) + n-1
= n-1
T(n) is in Θ(n). T(n) is linear.

5) Given a positive integer value n, algorithm computes the sum of the cubes of the first n positive integers, $1^3 + 2^3 + 3^3 + ... + n^3$.

```
//PRECONDITION n>0
int sumCubes(int n)
{
  if (n == 1)
    return 1;
  else
    return n*n*n + sumCubes(n-1);
}
```

ANALYSIS	
BASIC OPERATION:	*
PROBLEM SIZE:	n
RECURRENCE BASE CASE:	T(1) = 0
RECURRENCE RECURSIVE STEP:	T(n) = T(n-1) + 2

SOLVING RECURRENCE

T(1) = 0

T(n) = T(n-1) + 2, for n>1.
= (T(n-2) + 2) + 2 = T(n-2) + 4
= (T(n-3) + 2) + 4 = T(n-3) + 6
...
= T(n-(n-1)) + 2(n-1)
= T(1) + 2(n-1)
= 2n – 2

T(n) is in Θ(n). T(n) is linear.

6) Given a positive integer value n, algorithm computes the sum of the reciprocal values of the first n positive integers, 1/1 + 1/2 + 1/3 + ... + 1/n.

```
//PRECONDITION n>0
double harmonicSum(int n)
{
   if (n == 1)
     return 1.0;
   else
     return 1.0 / n + harmonicSum(n-1);
}
```

ANALYSIS	
BASIC OPERATION:	/
PROBLEM SIZE:	n
RECURRENCE BASE CASE:	T(1) = 0
RECURRENCE RECURSIVE STEP:	T(n) = T(n-1) + 1

SOLVING RECURRENCE

T(1) = 0
T(n) = T(n-1) + 1, for n>1.
= (T(n-2) + 1) + 1 = T(n-2) + 2
= (T(n-3) +1) + 2 = T(n-3) + 3
...
= T(n-(n-1)) + n-1
= T(1) + n-1
= n – 1
T(n) is in Θ(n). T(n) is linear.

7) Given a positive integer value n, write a method to compute the sum of the first n terms of the reciprocal values of the squares, $1/1^2 + 1/2^2 + 1/3^2 + ... + 1/n^2$.

```
//PRECONDITION n>0
double invnSquareSum(int n)
{
  if (n == 1)
    return 1.0;
  else
    return 1.0 / (n * n) + invnSquareSum(n-1);
}
```

ANALYSIS	
BASIC OPERATION:	/
PROBLEM SIZE:	n
RECURRENCE BASE CASE:	T(1) = 0
RECURRENCE RECURSIVE STEP:	T(n) = T(n-1) + 1

SOLVING RECURRENCE

$T(1) = 0$
$T(n) = T(n-1) + 1$, for $n>1$.
$= (T(n-2) + 1) + 1 = T(n-2) + 2$
$= (T(n-3) + 1) + 2 = T(n-3) + 3$
...
$= T(n-(n-1)) + n - 1$
$= T(1) + n - 1$
$= n - 1$

T(n) is in $\Theta(n)$. T(n) is linear.

8) Algorithm computes $1/1^3 + 1/2^3 + 1/3^3 + ... + 1/n^3$, the sum of the first n reciprocal values of cubes, for a given positive integer n.

```
//PRECONDITION n>0
double invCubesSum(int n)
{
  if (n == 1)
```

```
    return 1.0;
  else
    return 1.0 / (n*n*n) + invCubesSum(n-1);
}
```

ANALYSIS	
BASIC OPERATION:	*
PROBLEM SIZE:	n
RECURRENCE BASE CASE:	T(1) = 0
RECURRENCE RECURSIVE STEP:	T(n) = T(n-1) + 2

SOLVING RECURRENCE

$T(1) = 0$
$T(n) = T(n-1) + 2$, for $n>1$.
$= (T(n-2) + 2) + 2 = T(n-2) + 4$
$= (T(n-3) + 2) + 4 = T(n-3) + 6$
. . .
$= T(n-(n-1)) + 2(n-1)$
$= T(1) + 2n-2$
$= 2n - 2$

T(n) is in $\Theta(n)$. T(n) is linear.

9) Algorithm prints "Hello" n times. Assume that n is a positive integer.

```
//PRECONDITION n>0
void printHello(int n)
{
  if (n == 1)
    System.out.println("Hello");
  else
  {
    System.out.println("Hello");
    printHello(n - 1);
  }
}
```

ANALYSIS	
BASIC OPERATION:	System.out.println
PROBLEM SIZE:	n
RECURRENCE BASE CASE:	T(1) = 1
RECURRENCE RECURSIVE STEP:	T(n) = T(n-1) + 1, for n>1.

SOLVING RECURRENCE

T(1) = 1
T(n) = T(n-1) + 1, for n>1.
    = (T(n-2) + 1) + 1 = T(n-2) + 2
    = (T(n-3) + 1) + 2 = T(n-3) + 3
    . . .
    = T(n-(n-1)) + (n-1)
    = T(1) + n -1
    = 1 + n - 1
    = n

T(n) is in Θ(n). T(n) is linear.

10) Algorithm prints numbers from a positive integer number n down to 1. For instance, for n equal to 5 the printout is 5 4 3 2 1.

```
//PRECONDITION n>0
void print_nDownto1(int n)
{
  if (n == 1)
     System.out.print("1");
  else
  {
    System.out.print(n);
    print_nDownto1(n-1);
  }
}
```

ANALYSIS	
BASIC OPERATION:	System.out.print
PROBLEM SIZE:	n
RECURRENCE BASE CASE:	T(1) = 1
RECURRENCE RECURSIVE STEP:	T(n) = T(n-1) + 1, for n>1.

SOLVING RECURRENCE

T(1) = 1
T(n) = T(n-1) + 1, for n>1.
= (T(n-2) +1) + 1 = T(n-2) + 2
= (T(n-3) +1) + 2 = T(n-3) + 3
...
= T(n-(n-1)) + (n-1)
= T(1) + n-1 = 1 + n -1
= n

T(n) is in Θ(n). T(n) is linear.

11) Algorithm determines whether or not a given nonempty integer array of size n is sorted in increasing order.

```
//PRECONDITION:  n>0
public boolean isSortedArray(int[] list, int n)
{
  if (n == 1)
     return true;
  else if (list [n-1] >= list [n-2])
     return isSortedArray(list, n-1);
  else
     return false;
}
```

ANALYSIS	**Worst case analysis**
BASIC OPERATION:	Comparison of list elements
PROBLEM SIZE:	n
RECURRENCE BASE CASE:	T(1) = 0
RECURRENCE RECURSIVE STEP:	T(n) = T(n-1) + 1

SOLVING RECURRENCE

T(1) = 0
T(n) = T(n-1) + 1, for n>1.
= (T(n-2) + 1) + 1 = T(n-2) + 2
= (T(n-3) + 1) + 2 = T(n-3) + 3
...
= T(n-(n-1)) + n - 1
= T(1) + n - 1
= n – 1

T(n) is in Θ(n). T(n) is linear.

12) Algorithm computes the sum of all elements of a given nonempty integer array named list. Assume that the actual size of the list is n.

```
//PRECONDITION: n>0
public int sum(int[] list, int n)
{
   if (n == 1)
     return list[0];
   else
     return list[n-1] + sum(list, n-1);
}
```

ANALYSIS	
BASIC OPERATION:	+
PROBLEM SIZE:	n
RECURRENCE BASE CASE:	T(1) = 0
RECURRENCE RECURSIVE STEP:	T(n) = T(n-1) + 1, for n>1.

SOLVING RECURRENCE

T(1) = 0
T(n) = T(n-1) + 1, for n>1.
= (T(n-2) + 1) + 1 = T(n-2) + 2
= (T(n-3) + 1) + 2 = T(n-3) + 3
...
= T(n-(n-1)) + n - 1

= T(1) + n - 1
= n – 1

T(n) is in Θ(n). T(n) is linear.

13) Algorithm computes the product of all elements of the nonempty integer array list with actual size n.

```
//PRECONDITION n>0
public int product(int[] list, int n)
{
   if (n == 1)
     return list[0];
   else
     return list[n-1] * product(list, n-1);
}
```

ANALYSIS	
BASIC OPERATION:	*
PROBLEM SIZE:	n
RECURRENCE BASE CASE:	T(1) = 0
RECURRENCE RECURSIVE STEP:	T(n) = T(n-1) + 1, for n>1.

SOLVING RECURRENCE

T(1) = 0
T(n) = T(n-1) + 1, for n>1.
= (T(n-2) + 1) + 1 = T(n-2) + 2
= (T(n-3) + 1) + 2 = T(n-3) + 3
…
= T(n-(n-1)) + n - 1
= T(1) + n - 1
= n – 1

T(n) is in Θ(n). T(n) is linear.

14) Algorithm computes the number of elements having the same value as the variable item in an integer array list with size n.

```
//PRECONDITION n≥0
public int countItem(int[] list, int n, int item)
{
   if (n == 0)
     return 0;
   else if (list[n-1] == item)
     return 1 + countItem(list, n-1, item);
   else
     return countItem(list, n-1, item);
}
```

ANALYSIS	
BASIC OPERATION:	Comparison of a list element with item
PROBLEM SIZE:	n
RECURRENCE BASE CASE:	T(0) = 0
RECURRENCE RECURSIVE STEP:	T(n) = T(n-1) + 1

SOLVING RECURRENCE

T(0) = 0
T(n) = T(n-1) + 1, for n>0.
= (T(n-2) + 1) + 1 = T(n-2) + 2
= (T(n-3) + 1) + 2 = T(n-3) + 3
...
= T(n-n) + n
= T(0) + n
= n

T(n) is in Θ(n). T(n) is linear.

15) Algorithm computes the number of elements in an integer array list with actual size n that have positive values.

```
//PRECONDITION n≥0
public int countPositive(int[] list, int n)
{
  if (n == 0)
    return 0;
  else if (list[n-1] > 0)
```

```
    return  1 + countPositive(list, n-1);
  else
    return countPositive(list, n-1);
}
```

ANALYSIS	
BASIC OPERATION:	Comparison of list elements with zero
PROBLEM SIZE:	n
RECURRENCE BASE CASE:	T(0) = 0
RECURRENCE RECURSIVE STEP:	T(n) = T(n-1) + 1

SOLVING RECURRENCE

T(0) = 0
T(n) = T(n-1) + 1, for n>0.
= (T(n-2) + 1) + 1 = T(n-2) + 2
= (T(n-3) + 1) + 2 = T(n-3) + 3
...
= T(n-n) + n
= T(0) + n
= n

T(n) is in Θ(n). T(n) is linear.

16) Algorithm performs recursive selection sort on a given array list with n elements of type Comparable. Parameter n is actual size of the array list. List may be empty or not.

```
//PRECONDITION n≥0
public void selectionSort (Comparable[]  list, int n)
{
  Comparable temp;
  if (n > 1)
  {
     indexMax = 0;
     for (int i = 1; i < n; i++)                    //n-1 iterations
       if (list[i].compareTo( list[indexMax]) > 0)  //one basic op
          indexMax = i;
     temp = list[indexMax];
     list[indexMax] = list[n-1];
```

```
      list[n-1] = temp;
      selectionSort(list, n-1);
   }
}
```

ANALYSIS	
BASIC OPERATION:	Comparison of list elements
PROBLEM SIZE:	n
RECURRENCE BASE CASE:	T(0) = 0, T(1) = 0
RECURRENCE RECURSIVE STEP:	T(n) = T(n-1) + n-1

SOLVING RECURRENCE

T(0) = 0, T(1) = 0
T(n) = T(n-1) + (n-1), for n>1.
= (T(n-2) + (n-2)) + (n-1) = T(n-2) + (n-2) + (n-1)
= (T(n-3) + (n-3)) + (n-2) + (n-1) = T(n-3) + (n-3) + (n-2) + (n-1)
. . .
= T(n-(n-1)) + (n - (n – 1)) + . . . + (n-3) + (n-2) + (n-1)
= T(1) + 1 + 2 + . . . + (n-3) + (n-2) + (n-1)
= n (n – 1) / 2

T(n) is in $\Theta(n^2)$. T(n) is quadratic.

17) Algorithm performs insertion sort on a given integer array list with n occupied elements. Array may be either empty or not. Do worst case analysis.

```
//PRECONDITION n≥0
void insertionSort (int[] list, int n)
{
   int i, value;
   if ( n > 1 )
   {
      insertionSort( list, n-1 );
      value = list[n-1];
      i = n - 1;
      while (i > 0 && list[i-1] > value )
      {
```

```
            list[i] = list[i-1];
            i--;
        }
        list[i] = value;
    }
}
```

ANALYSIS	**Worst case analysis**
BASIC OPERATION:	Comparison of list elements
PROBLEM SIZE:	n
RECURRENCE BASE CASE:	T(0) = 0, T(1) = 0
RECURRENCE RECURSIVE STEP:	T(n) = T(n-1) + n-1

SOLVING RECURRENCE

T(0) = 0, T(1) = 0
T(n) = T(n-1) + (n-1), for n>1.
= (T(n-2) + (n-2)) + (n-1) = T(n-2) + (n-2) + (n-1)
= (T(n-3) + (n-3)) + (n-2) + (n-1) = T(n-3) + (n-3) + (n-2) + (n-1)
. . .
= T(n-(n-1)) + (n - (n - 1)) + . . . + (n-3) + (n-2) + (n-1)
= T(1) + 1 + 2 + . . . + (n-3) + (n-2) + (n-1)
= n (n - 1) / 2

T(n) is in $\Theta(n^2)$. T(n) is quadratic.

18) Algorithm performs recursive bubble sort on a given array list with n elements of type Comparable. Parameter n is actual size of the array list. List may be empty or not.

```
//PRECONDITION size≥0
public void bubbleSort(Comparable[] list, int n)
{
  int i, temp;
  if (n > 1)
  {
    for(i=0; i<n-1; i++)
    {
```

```
        if (list[i].compareTo (list[i+1])>0)
        {
           temp = list[i];
           list[i] = list[i+1];
           list[i+1] = temp;
        }
     }
     bubbleSort(list, n-1);
  }
}
```

ANALYSIS	
BASIC OPERATION:	Comparison of list elements
PROBLEM SIZE:	n
RECURRENCE BASE CASE:	T(0) = 0, T(1) = 0
RECURRENCE RECURSIVE STEP:	T(n) = T(n-1) + n-1

SOLVING RECURRENCE

$T(0) = 0, T(1) = 0$
$T(n) = T(n-1) + (n-1)$, for $n>1$.
$= (T(n-2) + (n-2)) + (n-1) = T(n-2) + (n-2) + (n-1)$
$= (T(n-3) + (n-3)) + (n-2) + (n-1) = T(n-3) + (n-3) + (n-2) + (n-1)$
. . .
$= T(n-(n-1)) + (n - (n - 1)) + \ldots + (n-3) + (n-2) + (n-1)$
$= T(1) + 1 + 2 + \ldots + (n-3) + (n-2) + (n-1)$
$= n(n - 1) / 2$

T(n) is in $\Theta(n^2)$. T(n) is quadratic.

19) Method returns true if array of integers is a palindrome and false otherwise.

```
public boolean isPalindrome(int[] numbers, int first, int last)
{
   if (first >= last)
     return true;
   else if ( numbers[first] != numbers[last])
     return false;
```

```
   else
      return isPalindrome(numbers, first+1, last-1);
}
```

ANALYSIS	
BASIC OPERATION:	Comparing array elements
PROBLEM SIZE:	n denoting last-first +1
RECURRENCE BASE CASE:	$T(0) = 0$, $T(1) = 0$
RECURRENCE RECURSIVE STEP:	$T(n) = T(n-2) + 1$

SOLVING RECURRENCE

$T(0) = 0$, $T(1) = 0$
$T(n) = T(n-2) + 1$, for $n>0$.

$= (T(n-4) + 1) + 1 = T(n-4) + 2$
$= (T(n-6) + 1) + 2 = T(n-6) + 3$
$= T(n-2k) + k$

for n even $k=n/2$
$= T(n-2n/2) + n/2$
$= T(0) + n/2$
$= n/2$

for n odd $k=(n-1)/2$
$= T(n-2(n-1)/2) + (n-1)/2$
$= T(1) + (n-1)/2$
$= (n-1)/2$

$T(n)$ is in $\Theta(n)$. $T(n)$ is linear.

20) Accepts one digit positive integer n and returns ArrayList of String type of all permutations of numbers 1,2,…,n. Use adding one permutation to the result as a basic operation.

```
//PRECONDITION n>0
ArrayList<String> permutations(int n)
{
  ArrayList<String> result, oldResult;
  String current;
  result = new ArrayList<String>();
  if (n == 1)
  {
     result.add("1");
     return result;
  }
  else
```

```
  {
    oldResult = permutations(n-1);          // subproblem time is T(n-1)
    for(String oldCurrent: oldResult)       // loop has (n-1)! iterations
    {
      result.add(n + oldCurrent);           // one basic op
      for(int j = 0; j<n-1; j++)            // n-1 iterations with one basic op
      {
         current = oldCurrent.substring(0,j+1) + n +
                   oldCurrent.substring(j+1,n-1 );
         result.add(current);
      }
    }
    return result;
  }
}
```

ANALYSIS	
BASIC OPERATION:	Adding one permutation to the result
PROBLEM SIZE:	n
RECURRENCE BASE CASE:	T(1) = 1
RECURRENCE RECURSIVE STEP:	T(n) = T(n-1) + n!

SOLVING RECURRENCE

$T(1) = 1$
$T(n) = T(n-1) + n!$, for $n>1$.
$= T(n-2) + (n-1)! + n!$
$= T(n-3) + (n-2)! + (n-1)! + n!$
...
$= T(n-(n-1)) + (n - (n-2))! + \ldots + (n-3)! + (n-2)! + (n-1)! + n!$
$= T(1) + 2! + \ldots + (n-1)! + n!$
$= 1! + 2! + 3! + \ldots + n! = \sum_{i=1}^{n} i!$ =Kurepa(n)

NOTE: Late professor Kurepa has introduced a function which he called left factorial and denoted $!n = \sum_{i=0}^{n-1} i!$ The relationship between !n and Kurepa (n) is Kurepa(n) = !n + n! -1

T(n) is in $\Omega(n!)$. T(n) grows much faster than n!.

21) Algorithm accepts one-digit positive integer n and returns ArrayList of all subsets of the set {1,2,...,n}. Denote empty set as 0. Use adding current subset to the result as a basic operation.

```
//PRECONDITION n>0
ArrayList<String> powerSet(int n)
{
  ArrayList<String> result, oldResult;
  String current;
  result = new ArrayList<String>();
  if(n == 0)
    result.add("0");
  else
  {
     oldResult = powerSet(n-1);              // recursive call time: T(n-1)
     for(String oldCurrent: oldResult)       // iterates 2^(n-1) times
       result.add(oldCurrent);               // one basic op each iteration
     for(String oldCurrent: oldResult)       // iterates 2^(n-1) times
       if (oldCurrent != "0")
         result.add(oldCurrent+", " + n);     // one basic operation
       else
         result.add("" + n);                  // one basic operation
  }
  return result;
}
```

ANALYSIS

BASIC OPERATION:	Calling add method to add to the result
PROBLEM SIZE:	n
RECURRENCE BASE CASE:	T(0) = 1
RECURRENCE RECURSIVE STEP:	T(n) = T(n-1) + 2^n, for n>0.

SOLVING RECURRENCE

T(0) = 1

T(n) = T(n-1) + 2^n, for n>0.

= T(n-2) + 2^{n-1}+ 2^n

= T(n-3) + 2^{n-2}+ 2^{n-1}+ 2^n

= T(n-n) + $2^{n-(n-1)}$+ ...+ 2^{n-3} + 2^{n-2}+ 2^{n-1}+ 2^n

= T(0) + $\sum_{i=1}^{n} 2^i$

$= \sum_{i=0}^{n} 2^i$
$= 2^{n+1}-1$

T(n) is in $\Theta(2^n)$. T(n) is exponential.

22) Algorithm prints one letter if n is zero. For n larger than zero it calls subproblem of size n-1, and prints 2^n letters.

```
//PRECONDITION n>=0
public int printLetters(int n)
{
   if (n == 0)
     System.out.print ("A");
   else
   {
     printLetters(n - 1);
     for(int i=1; i<=Math.pow(2, n); i++)
       System.out.print ("A");
   }
}
```

ANALYSIS

BASIC OPERATION:	Printing one letter "A"
PROBLEM SIZE:	n
RECURRENCE BASE CASE:	T(0) = 1
RECURRENCE RECURSIVE STEP:	$T(n) = T(n-1) + 2^n$

SOLVING RECURRENCE

T(0) = 1
$T(n) = T(n-1) + 2^n$, for n>0.

$= T(n-2) + 2^{n-1} + 2^n$
$= T(n-3) + 2^{n-2} + 2^{n-1} + 2^n$
$= T(n-n) + 2^{n-(n-1)} + ... + 2^{n-3} + 2^{n-2} + 2^{n-1} + 2^n$
$= T(0) + \sum_{i=1}^{n} 2^i$
$= \sum_{i=0}^{n} 2^i$

$= 2^{n+1}-1$

T(n) is in $\Theta(2^n)$. T(n) is exponential.

23) Algorithm draws n letters "l" in the same row on a graphical surface as shown on the picture bellow. Variable n is a positive integer.

Applet Viewer: PrintLetterLinear.class

Applet

| | | | | | | | | | | | | | | | | | | | | | | | |

Applet started.

```
public final int HDIST=10;
public final int VDIST=20;

public void rec( int n, Graphics g)
{
  if (n==1)
    g.drawString("l", HDIST, VDIST);
  else
  {
    g.drawString("l", n*HDIST, VDIST);
    rec(n-1, g);
  }
}
```

ANALYSIS

BASIC OPERATION:	Draw one letter "l" on a graphical surface
PROBLEM SIZE:	n
RECURRENCE BASE CASE:	T(1) = 1
RECURRENCE RECURSIVE STEP:	T(n) = T(n-1) + 1, for n>1

SOLVING RECURRENCE

T(1) = 1
T(n) = T(n-1) + 1, for n>1.

$= (T(n-2) + 1) + 1 = T(n-2) + 2$
$= (T(n-3) + 1) + 2 = T(n-3) + 3$
...
$= T(n-(n-1)) + (n-1)$
$= T(1) + n - 1$
$= 1 + n - 1$
$= n$

T(n) is in $\Theta(n)$. T(n) is linear.

24) Algorithm draws spiral on the graphical surface.

Basic operation is drawing one pixel on a graphical surface. Problem size is n, which is also the length of the longest horizontal line. Each next line rotates clockwise by 90 degrees and its length is decreased by DIST. Stopping case is when line length is shorter than DIST.

```
public final int DIST=4;

public void spiralRec(int x, int y, int n, int to, Graphics g)
{
   if (n >= DIST)
   {
      if ( to % DIST == 0) // move right
```

```
        {
           g.drawLine( x, y, x+n-1, y ); //line of length n
           spiralRec(x + n-1, y, n-DIST, (to+1)% DIST, g);
        }
        else if ( to % DIST == 1) // move down
        {
           g.drawLine( x, y, x, y+n-1 ); //line of length n
           spiralRec(x, y+n-1, n-DIST, (to+1)% DIST, g);
        }
        else if ( to % DIST == 2) // move left
        {
           g.drawLine( x, y, x-n+1, y ); //line of length n
           spiralRec(x-n+1, y, n-DIST, (to+1)% DIST, g);
        }
        else if ( to % DIST == 3) // move up
        {
           g.drawLine( x, y, x, y-n+1 ); //line of length n
           spiralRec(x, y-n+1, n-DIST, (to+1)% DIST, g);
        }
    }
}
```

ANALYSIS	
BASIC OPERATION:	Drawing one pixel on a graphical surface
PROBLEM SIZE:	n
RECURRENCE BASE CASE:	T(0) = 0, T(1) = 0, T(2) = 0, T(3) = 0
RECURRENCE RECURSIVE STEP:	T(n) = T(n-4) + n, for all n>=4.

SOLVING RECURRENCE

T(0) = 0, T(1) = 0, T(2) = 0, T(3) = 0

T(n) = T(n-4) + n, for n>3. Assume that n is 4k.

= (T(n-8) + (n-4)) + n = T(n-8) + (n-4) + n

= T(n-12) + (n-8) + (n-4) + n

. . .

= T(n-4k) + (n-(4k-4)) + (n-(4k-8)) + . . . + (n-8) + (n-4) + n

= T(n-4k) + 4 + 8 + . . . + (n-8) + (n-4) + n

= T(0) +4 $\sum_{i=1}^{k} i$

= 4 k(k+1)/2
= 2 k(k+1)
=2(n/4)(n/4 + 1)= n (n/4 + 1) / 2 = n(n + 4) / 8

T(n) is in $\Theta(n^2)$. Running time is quadratic.

25-26) Algorithm draws vertical parallel lines that are one pixel apart from each other. Each next line is DIST pixels shorter than the previous one and has an x coordinate of DIST pixels less.

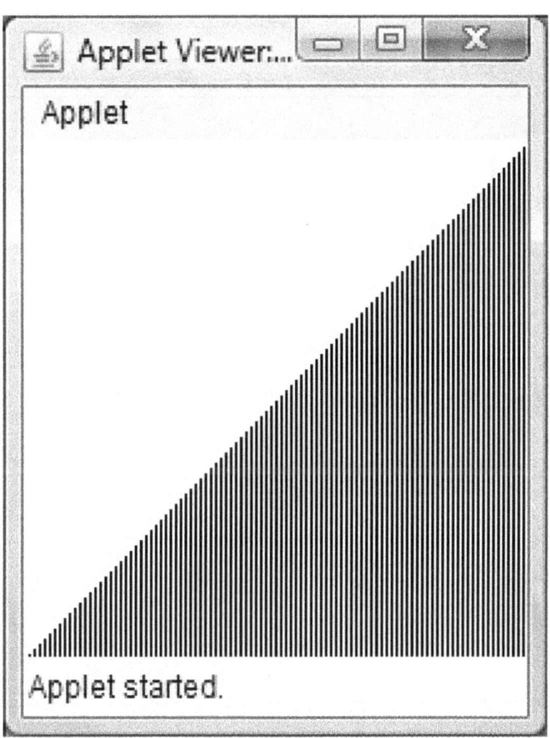

All bottom points for the lines have y coordinate equal to SIZE. Top points have y coordinates that are decreasing by DIST. Picture shows resulting lines for DIST=2 and DIST=1. Perform analysis for both cases.

```
public final int SIZE=200;              //applet's width and height
public final int DIST=2;                //DIST=1 for second example
public void recVLinesDec(int n, Graphics g)
{
  if (n>=0)
  {
    g.drawLine(n,SIZE-n+1,n,SIZE);    //line length is equal to n
```

```
    recVLinesDec(n-DIST, g);
   }
}
```

ANALYSIS

BASIC OPERATION:	Drawing one pixel on graphical surface
PROBLEM SIZE:	n
RECURRENCE BASE CASE:	T(0) = 0
RECURRENCE RECURSIVE STEP:	T(n) = T(n-DIST) + n

SOLVING RECURRENCE

T(0) = 0
T(n) = T(n-DIST) + n
= T(n-2DIST) + (n-DIST) + n
= T(n-3DIST) + (n-2DIST) + (n-DIST) + n
= T(n-4DIST) + (n-3DIST) + (n-2DIST) + (n-DIST) + n
= T(n-5DIST) +(n-4DIST) + (n-3DIST) + (n-2DIST) + (n-DIST) + n
. . .
= T(n-kDIST) + kn –DIST(1+2+3+ . . . +(k-1)) Let n=k DIST and k = n/DIST
= T(n-n) +kn -DIST $\sum_{i=1}^{k-1} i$
= T(0) + n^2/DIST-DIST k(k-1)/2= $2n^2$/(2DIST) - n^2/(2DIST) + n/(2DIST) = $\frac{n^2 - n\ DIST}{2DIST}$

Solution for DIST=2 T(n) = (n^2-2 n)/4.

Solution for DIST=1 T(n) = (n^2-n)/2.

T(n) is in $\Theta(n^2)$. It has quadratic asymptotic growth in both cases.

27) Use drawString method to draw letters "l" on a graphical surface as shown on the picture bellow. For given n there are n-1 rows. First row has n-1 letters, and each next row has one letter "l" less.

Problem size is n. Basic operation is drawing one letter "l" on the graphical surface. Recursive method `rec` has input parameter n which determines the depth of recursive calls. If n is either 0 or 1 nothing is done. For n greater than one, the nonrecursive part draws n-1 letter "l"s, and makes one call to recursive subproblem which has its size reduced to n-1.

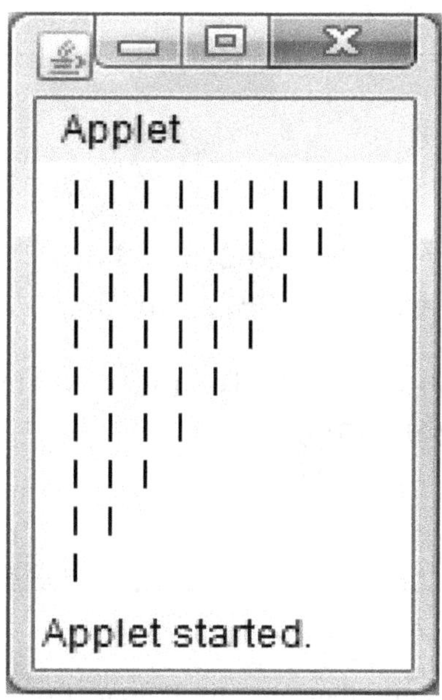


```
public final int VDIST=20;
public final int DIST=10;

public void printNletters(int n, int top, Graphics g)
{
   for(int i=1; i<=n; i++)
     g.drawString("l", i*DIST, top);
}

public void rec( int n, int y, Graphics g)
{
   if (n>1)
   {
     printNletters(n-1, y, g);
     rec(n-1, y+VDIST, g);
   }
}
```

ANALYSIS

BASIC OPERATION:	*
PROBLEM SIZE:	n
RECURRENCE BASE CASE:	$T(0) = 0, \quad T(1)=0$
RECURRENCE RECURSIVE STEP:	$T(n) = T(n-1) + n-1$

SOLVING RECURRENCE

$T(0) = 0, T(1) = 0$
$T(n) = T(n-1) + (n-1)$, for $n>1$.
$= (T(n-2) + (n-2)) + (n-1) = T(n-2) + (n-2) + (n-1)$
$= (T(n-3) + (n-3)) + (n-2) + (n-1) = T(n-3) + (n-3) + (n-2) + (n-1)$
...
$= T(n-(n-1)) + (n - (n - 1)) + \ldots + (n-3) + (n-2) + (n-1)$
$= T(1) + 1 + 2 + \ldots + (n-3) + (n-2) + (n-1)$
$= n (n - 1) / 2$

$T(n)$ is in $\Theta(n^2)$. It is quadratic.

28) Draw concentric squares that are DIST apart from each other, as shown.

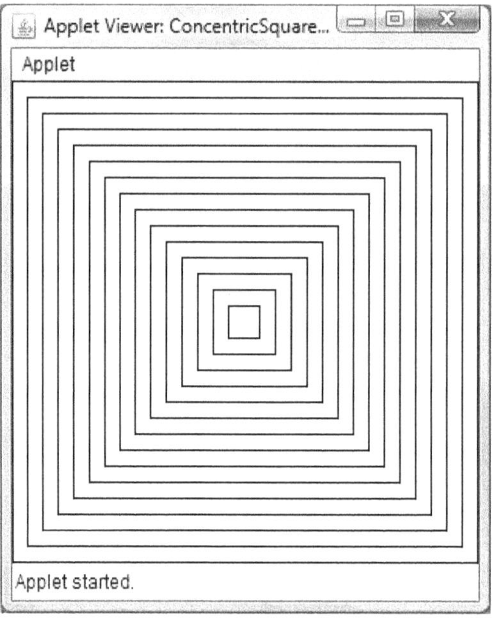

The largest square has side length n. Each next square has side length reduced by 2*DIST (because it is DIST less on both ends). Nonrecursive cost is drawing the largest square which requires 4n pixels. Recursive subproblem has size n reduced by 2*DIST.

```
public final int SIZE = 300;
public final int DIST = 10;

public void recSquare(int n, Graphics g)
```

```
{
    if (n > 0)
    {
       g.drawRect((SIZE-n)/2, (SIZE-n)/2, n, n);
       recSquare( n-2*DIST, g);
    }
}
```

ANALYSIS

BASIC OPERATION:	Drawing one pixel on the surface
PROBLEM SIZE:	n
RECURRENCE BASE CASE:	T(0) = 0
RECURRENCE RECURSIVE STEP:	T(n) = T(n-2DIST) + 4n

SOLVING RECURRENCE

T(0) = 0
T(n) = T(n-2DIST) + 4n, for n>0.
= T(n-4DIST) + 4(n-2DIST) + 4n
= T(n-6DIST) + 4(n-4DIST) + 4(n-2DIST) + 4n
...
= T(n-n) + 4(2DIST+ 4DIST + 6DIST + ... + n)
= T(0) + 4(2DIST+ 4DIST + 6DIST + ... + n)
= 4*2DIST*(1 + 2 + ... + n/2DIST)
= 4*2DIST *(n/2DIST) *(n/2DIST+1)/2
= 2n (n /2DIST+ 1)
= n(n+2DIST) / DIST

T(n) is in $\Theta(n^2)$. T(n) is quadratic.

CHAPTER 2

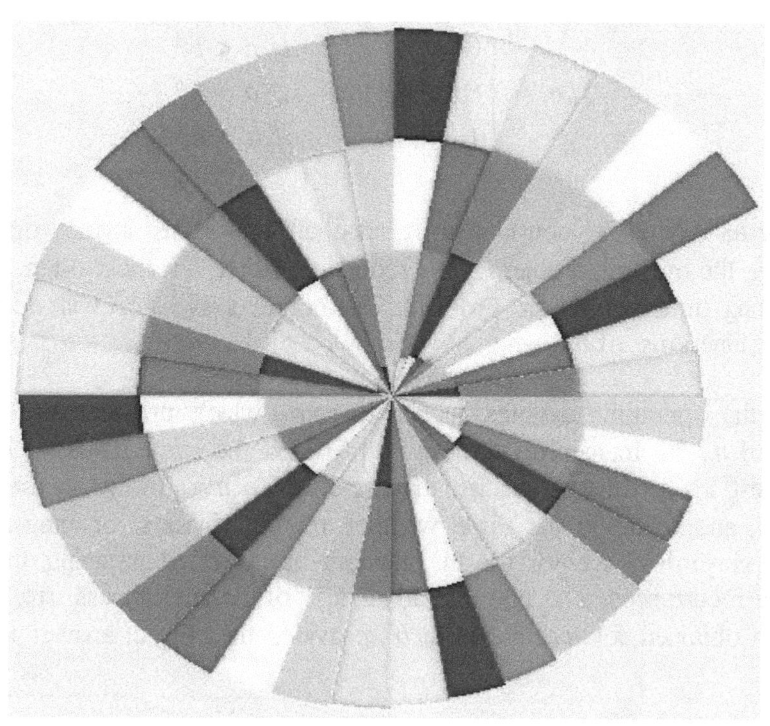

RUNNING TIME ANALYSIS OF DECREASE-BY-CONSTANT-FACTOR RECURSIVE ALGORITHMS

Recurrences type: $T(n) = T(n/b) + f(n)$.

Constant b is positive, and function f(n) is nonrecursive cost.

This chapter includes examples of running time analysis of decrease-by-constant-factor type algorithms. It covers problems of size n that invoke one sub-problem of size *n* reduced by factor *b*. Constant *b* is a positive integer that is larger than one. The corresponding recurrences for running time analysis are of type $T(n) = T(n / b) + f(n)$. Function $f(n)$ denotes the cost of the non-recursive portion of the code.

The Master Theorem is an important tool for determining asymptotic behavior of $T(n)$ for all decrease-by-constant-factor type problems discussed in this chapter as well as divide-and-conquer type problems that will be discussed in chapter 2. So, we provide the Master Theorem here in its general form for all problems with corresponding recurrences of the type $T(n) = a\,T(n / b) + f(n)$. Constants a and b satisfy constraints $a >= 1$ and $b > 1$.

Master Theorem If $f(n)$ is in $\Theta(n^d)$ where $d >= 0$ in recurrence $T(n) = a\,T(n / b) + f(n)$ then

$$\mathbf{T(n)} = \begin{cases} \Theta(n^d) & if\ a < b^d \\ \Theta(n^d \log n) & if\ a = b^d \\ \Theta(n^{\log_b a}) & if\ a > b^d \end{cases}$$

In this chapter, for all examples, constant a=1, since all algorithms invoke only one recursive subproblem to solve the original problem. The reduction factor *b* is most often 2, but sometimes it is 3 or 10 depending on the particular problem. The nonrecursive cost will be mostly constant, linear, or quadratic functions of *n*.

In all recurrences the operator / denotes integer division which provides the integer part of the standard division of n / b. Integer division n / b provides the same result as floor(n/b) which is defined as the largest integer that is smaller than or equal to n/b. In the special case where $n=b^k$, n is divisible by b, and so n/b is the same whether regular division or integer division is used. Without losing the generality, we will use the standard approach of assuming that $n = b^k$, for some k when solving the recurrences, and take the advantage of the smoothness rule which proves that the order of growth obtained for n of the form b^k, provides the correct answer for all values of n.

EXAMPLES

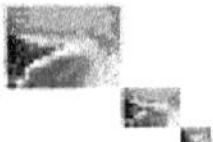

1) Algorithm prints a positive number n, represented in base 10 (decimal), converted to base 2 (binary notation).

```
//PRECONDITION: n positive
void convert(int n)
{
   if (n > 0)
   {
     convert(n / 2);
```

```
      System.out.print(n % 2);
    }
}
```

ANALYSIS	
BASIC OPERATION:	%
PROBLEM SIZE:	n
RECURRENCE BASE CASE:	T(1) = 1,
RECURRENCE RECURSIVE STEP:	T(n) = T(n/2) + 1, for n>1.

SOLVING RECURRENCE

$T(1) = 1,$
$T(n) = T(n/2) + 1, \text{ for } n>1.$
Assume that $n = 2^k$, and so, $k = \lg n$.

$$
\begin{aligned}
T(2^k) &= T(2^{k-1}) + 1 \\
&= (T(2^{k-2}) + 1) + 1 = T(2^{k-2}) + 2 \\
&= (T(2^{k-3}) + 1) + 2 = T(2^{k-3}) + 3 \\
&\ldots \\
&= T(2^{k-k}) + k = T(2^0) + k \\
&= T(1) + k \\
T(2^k) &= k + 1
\end{aligned}
$$

$T(n) = \lg n + 1$

T(n) is in $\Theta(\lg n)$. Running time is logarithmic.

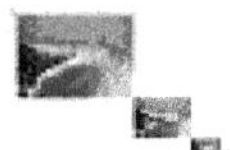

2) Algorithm returns the number of binary digits of a given nonnegative number n's binary representation.

```
// PRECONDITION: n is nonnegative
int binaryDigits(int n)
{
   if (n <= 1)
     return 1;
   else
     return  1 + binaryDigits(n/2);
}
```

ANALYSIS	
BASIC OPERATION:	+
PROBLEM SIZE:	n
RECURRENCE BASE CASE:	$T(0) = 0$, $T(1) = 0$,
RECURRENCE RECURSIVE STEP:	$T(n) = T(n/2) + 1$, for $n>1$.

SOLVING RECURRENCE

$T(0) = 0$, $T(1) = 0$
$T(n) = T(n/2) + 1$, for $n>1$.

Assume that n is 2^k. Consequently, $k = \lg n$.

$$
\begin{aligned}
T(2^k) &= T(2^{k-1}) + 1 \\
&= (T(2^{k-2}) + 1) + 1 = T(2^{k-2}) + 2 \\
&= (T(2^{k-3}) + 1) + 2 = T(2^{k-3}) + 3 \\
&\ldots \\
&= T(2^{k-k}) + k \\
&= T(1) + k \\
T(2^k) &= k \\
T(n) &= \lg n
\end{aligned}
$$

$T(n)$ is in $\Theta(\log n)$. Running time is logarithmic.

3) For a given sorted list of integers, algorithm returns the index of the element that equals the given item, or it returns -1 if none of the elements equals the item. Parameters first and last are indices of the first and last positions in the current subarray of the list. Perform worst case analysis.

PRECONDITION: list is sorted, and first<=last.

```
int binarySearch(int[] list, int first, int last, int item)
{
   if (first>last)
      return -1;
   else
   {
      int mid = (first + last)/2;
      if (item == list[mid])
         return mid;
      else if (item < list[mid])
```

```
            return binarySearch(list, first, mid-1, item);
        else
            return binarySearch(list, mid+1, last, item);
    }
}
```

ANALYSIS	Worst case analysis
BASIC OPERATION:	Comparison of list elements with item
PROBLEM SIZE:	n which denotes last-first+1
RECURRENCE BASE CASE:	$T(1) = 1$,
RECURRENCE RECURSIVE STEP:	$T(n) = T(n/2) + 2$, for $n>1$.

SOLVING RECURRENCE

$T(1) = 1$
$T(n) = T(n/2) + 2$, for $n>1$.

Assume that n is 2^k, and consequently $k = \lg n$.

$$\begin{aligned} T(2^k) &= T(2^{k-1}) + 2 \\ &= (T(2^{k-2}) + 2) + 2 = T(2^{k-2}) + 4 \\ &= (T(2^{k-3}) + 2) + 4 = T(2^{k-3}) + 6 \\ &\quad \ldots \\ &= T(2^{k-k}) + 2k \\ &= T(1) + 2k \end{aligned}$$

$T(2^k) = 2k + 1$
$T(n) = 2\lg n + 1$

$T(n)$ is in $\Theta(\log n)$. Running time is logarithmic.

4) For a given nonnegative integer number *n*, specified in base 10, algorithm returns a string of binary digits for *n*'s base 2 representation.

```
// PRECONDITION: n >=0.
String convertFromBase10To2(int n)
{
   String result;
   if (n<=1)
```

```
      result = "" + n;
   else
      result = convertFromBase10To2(n/2) + n%2;
   return result;
}
```

ANALYSIS	
BASIC OPERATION:	+ (string concatenation)
PROBLEM SIZE:	n
RECURRENCE BASE CASE:	T(0) = 1, T(1) = 1,
RECURRENCE RECURSIVE STEP:	T(n) = T(n/2) + 1, for all n>1.

SOLVING RECURRENCE

$T(0) = 1,\ T(1) = 1$
$T(n) = T(n/2) + 1,\ \text{for } n>1.$

Assume that n is 2^k, and consequently $k = \lg n$.

$$
\begin{aligned}
T(2^k) &= T(2^{k-1}) + 1 \\
&= (T(2^{k-2}) + 1) + 1 = T(2^{k-2}) + 2 \\
&= (T(2^{k-3}) + 1) + 2 = T(2^{k-3}) + 3 \\
&\ \ \cdots \\
&= T(2^{k-k}) + k \\
&= T(1) + k
\end{aligned}
$$

$T(2^k) = k + 1$
$T(n) = \lg n + 1$

T(n) is in $\Theta(\log n)$. Running time is logarithmic.

5) Algorithm displays the digits of a given nonnegative integer value n in reverse order.

```
// PRECONDITION: n >=0.
void printReverse(int n)
{
  if (n <= 9)
     System.out.print(n);
```

```
   else
   {
      System.out.print(n % 10);
      printReverse(n / 10);
   }
}
```

ANALYSIS	
BASIC OPERATION:	%
PROBLEM SIZE:	n
RECURRENCE BASE CASE:	$T(i) = 0$, for $0 \leq i \leq 9$
RECURRENCE RECURSIVE STEP:	$T(n) = T(n/10) + 1$, for all $n \geq 10$.

SOLVING RECURRENCE

$T(i) = 0$, for $0 \leq i \leq 9$
$T(n) = T(n/10) + 1$, for all $n > 9$.

Assume that $n = 10^k$, and consequently $k = \log_{10} n$.

$$
\begin{aligned}
T(n) &= T(n/10) + 1 \\
&= (T(n/10^2) + 1) + 1 = T(n/10^2) + 2 \\
&= (T(n/10^3) + 1) + 2 = T(n/10^3) + 3 \\
&\ldots \\
&= T(n/10^k) + k \\
&= T(1) + k \\
&= k \\
T(n) &= \log_{10} n
\end{aligned}
$$

$T(n)$ is in $\Theta(\log n)$. Running time is logarithmic.

6) Algorithm returns the number of digits in an integer n. Number n is represented in base ten.

```
// PRECONDITION: n nonnegative integer
int numberOfDigits(int n)
{
  if (n <= 9)
    return 1;
```

```
  else
    return 1 + numberOfDigits(n / 10);
}
```

ANALYSIS	
BASIC OPERATION:	/
PROBLEM SIZE:	n
RECURRENCE BASE CASE:	$T(i) = 0$, for $0 \le i \le 9$
RECURRENCE RECURSIVE STEP:	$T(n) = T(n/10) + 1$, for all $n \ge 10$.

SOLVING RECURRENCE

$T(j) = 0$, for $0 \le j \le 9$
$T(n) = T(n/10) + 1$, for all $n \ge 10$.

Assume that n is 10^k, and consequently, $k = \log_{10} n$.

$$
\begin{aligned}
T(n) &= T(n/10) + 1 = (T(n/10^2) + 1) + 1 \\
&= T(n/10^2) + 1 + 1 = (T(n/10^3) + 1) + 1 + 1 \\
&= T(n/10^3) + 1 + 1 + 1 \\
&\dots \\
&= T(n/10^k) + k \\
&= T(1) + k \\
&= k \\
T(n) &= \log_{10} n
\end{aligned}
$$

$T(n)$ is in $\Theta(\log n)$. Running time is logarithmic.

7) For a nonnegative integer number *n*, specified in base 10, algorithm returns a string of digits for *n*'s base 3 representation.

```
// PRECONDITION: n>=0
String convert10To3(int n)
{
   String result;
   if (n <= 2)
      result = "" + n;
   else
      result = convert10To3(n/3) + n%3;
```

```
   return result;
}
```

ANALYSIS	
BASIC OPERATION:	+ (string concatenation)
PROBLEM SIZE:	n
RECURRENCE BASE CASE:	$T(0) = 1,\ T(1) = 1,\ T(2) = 1$
RECURRENCE RECURSIVE STEP:	$T(n) = T(n/3) + 1$, for all $n>2$.

SOLVING RECURRENCE

$T(0) = 1,\ T(1) = 1,\ T(2) = 1$
$T(n) = T(n/3) + 1$, for $n>2$.

Assume that n is 3^k, and consequently $k = \log_3 n$.

$$
\begin{aligned}
T(3^k) &= T(3^{k-1}) + 1 = (T(3^{k-2}) + 1) + 1 \\
&= T(3^{k-2}) + 2 = (T(3^{k-3}) + 1) + 2 \\
&= T(3^{k-3}) + 3 \\
&\ldots \\
&= T(3^{k-k}) + k \\
&= T(1) + k \\
T(3^k) &= k + 1 \\
T(n) &= \log_3 n + 1
\end{aligned}
$$

T(n) is in $\Theta(\log n)$. Running time is logarithmic.

8) For a given positive integer number $n>1$, algorithm prints letter 'A' $\log_2 n$ times by calling one recursive subproblem of size $n/2$. (Use n of the form 2^k to test it.)

PRECONDITION: n>0

```
void printLog (int n)
{
   if (n>1)
   {
     System.out.print("A");
```

```
      printLog(n/2);
    }
}
```

ANALYSIS	
BASIC OPERATION:	Print letter "A"
PROBLEM SIZE:	n
RECURRENCE BASE CASE:	T(0) = 0, T(1) = 0,
RECURRENCE RECURSIVE STEP:	T(n) = T(n/2) + 1, for all n>1.

SOLVING RECURRENCE

$T(0) = 0, \; T(1) = 0$
$T(n) = T(n/2) + 1$, for n>1.

Assume that n is 2^k, and consequently, $k = \lg n$.

$$
\begin{aligned}
T(2^k) &= T(2^{k-1}) + 1 = (T(2^{k-2}) + 1) + 1 \\
&= T(2^{k-2}) + 2 = (T(2^{k-3}) + 1) + 2 \\
&= T(2^{k-3}) + 3 \\
&\;\;\ldots \\
&= T(2^{k-k}) + k \\
&= T(1) + k
\end{aligned}
$$

$T(2^k) \;\; = k$
$T(n) \;\;\; = \lg n$

T(n) is in $\Theta(\log n)$. Running time is logarithmic.

9) Algorithm computes d^n for a non-negative integer n and a real number d. The following definitions are used. If n is 0, $d^0 = 1$. If n is positive and even, $d^n = d^{(n/2)} * d^{(n/2)}$. If n is positive and odd, $d^n = d * d^{(n/2)} * d^{(n/2)}$. Only one subproblem of size $n/2$ is called in the code. Analyze best case performance when $n=2^k$ and k is a positive integer.

```
// PRECONDITION: d ≠ 0
public double power(double d, int n)
{
  if (n == 0)
    return 1;
```

```
  else if (n == 1)
    return d;
  {
    double temp = power(d, n/2);
    if (n % 2 == 1)
      return d * temp * temp;
    else
      return temp * temp;
  }
}
```

ANALYSIS	Best case analysis
BASIC OPERATION:	*
PROBLEM SIZE:	n
RECURRENCE BASE CASE:	$T(0) = 0,\ T(1) = 0$
RECURRENCE RECURSIVE STEP:	$T(n) = T(n/2) + 1$, for all n>1.

SOLVING RECURRENCE

$T(0) = 0,\ T(1) = 0$
$T(n) = T(n/2) + 1$, for n>1.

Assume that n is 2^k, and consequently $k = \lg n$.

$$\begin{aligned} T(2^k) &= T(2^{k-1}) + 1 \\ &= (T(2^{k-2}) + 1) + 1 = T(2^{k-2}) + 2 \\ &= (T(2^{k-3}) + 1) + 2 = T(2^{k-3}) + 3 \\ &\dots \\ &= T(2^{k-k}) + k = T(2^0) + k \\ &= T(1) + k \end{aligned}$$

$T(2^k) = k$
$T(n) = \lg n$

$T(n)$ is in $\Theta(\log n)$. Running time is logarithmic.

10) Algorithm draws a spiral on the graphical surface as shown. The length of the adjacent line segments decrease by half in a clockwise direction.

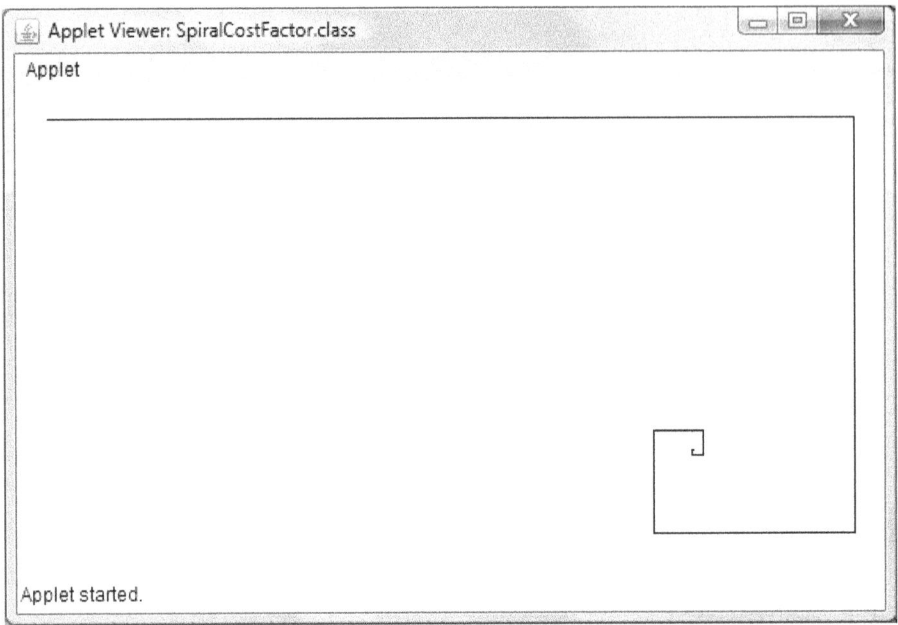

// PRECONDITION: n>0.

```
public void spiralRec(int x, int y, int n, int to, Graphics g)
{
  if (n > 1)
  {
    if ( to % 4 == 0)                                // move right
    {
      g.drawLine( x, y, x + n-1, y );                //n pixels long
      spiralRec(x + n - 1, y, n/2, (to + 1)%4, g);
    }
    else if ( to % 4 == 1)                           // move down
    {
      g.drawLine( x, y, x, y + n - 1 );              //n pixels long
      spiralRec(x, y + n - 1, n/2, (to + 1)%4, g);
    }
    else if ( to % 4 == 2)                           // move left
    {
      g.drawLine(x, y, x - n + 1, y);                //n pixels long
      spiralRec(x - n + 1, y, n/2, (to + 1)%4, g);

    }
    else if ( to % 4 == 3)                           // move up
    {
```

```
        g.drawLine( x, y, x, y - n + 1);          //n pixels long
        spiralRec( x, y - n + 1, n/2, (to + 1) % 4, g);
      }
   }
}
```

ANALYSIS	
BASIC OPERATION:	Drawing one pixel on a graphical surface
PROBLEM SIZE:	n
RECURRENCE BASE CASE:	T(1) = 0,
RECURRENCE RECURSIVE STEP:	T(n) = T(n/2) + n, for all n>1.

SOLVING RECURRENCE

$T(1) = 0$
$T(n) = T(n/2) + n$, for $n>1$.

Assume that n is 2^k.

$T(n) = T(n/2) + n$
$= (T(n/2^2) + n/2\ ) + n = T(n/2^2) + n/2 + n$
$= (T(n/2^3) + n/2^2\ ) + n/2 + n = T(n/2^3) + n/2^2 + n/2^1 + n/2^0$
. . .
$= T(n/2^k) + n\,(1/2^{k-1} + 1/2^{k-2} + \ldots + 1/2^2 + 1/2^1 + 1/2^0)$

$= T(1) + n\sum_{i=0}^{k-1} \frac{1}{2^i}$

$= 0 + n\ \frac{(\frac{1}{2})^k - 1}{-\frac{1}{2}}$

$= 2^k\ \frac{(\frac{1}{2})^k - 1}{-\frac{1}{2}}$

$= (1 - 2^k)/(-\frac{1}{2})$
$= 2(2^k - 1)$
$= 2n - 2$

T(n) is in $\Theta(n)$. Running time is linear function of n.

11) Algorithm draws squares as shown. Each square has a side one half the length of the side of the previous square, and its upper left corner is in the upper right corner of the previous square.

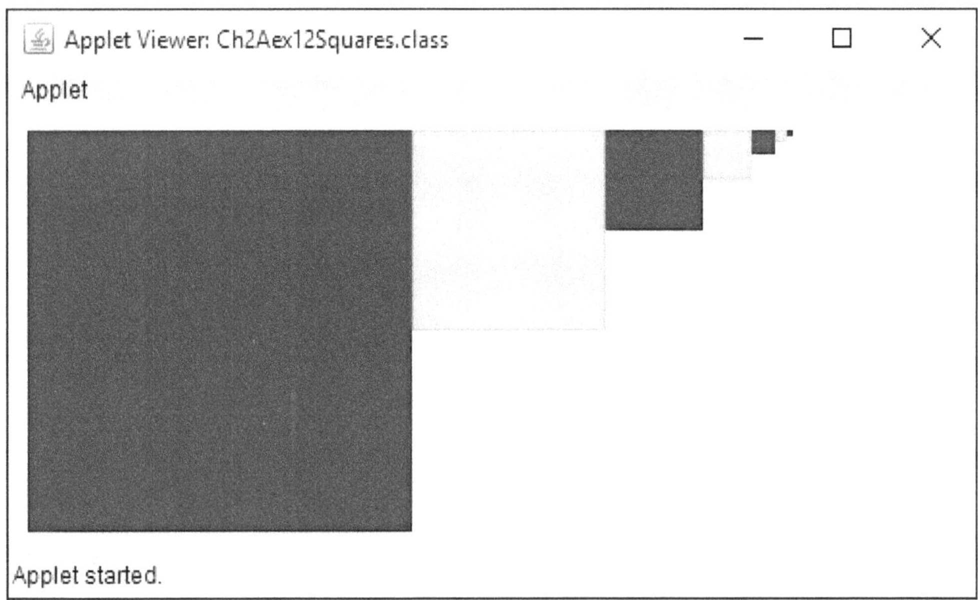

At the highest level of recursion the square with the upper left corner at x,y, and size n x n is drawn with the specified color. In addition, one recursive call is made. Parameter n is reduced to n/2 and x,y for the new upper left corner is moved n pixels to the right from the left upper corner of the largest square.

```
public void recSquares(int x, int y, int n, int c, Graphics g)
{
 if ( n > 1)
 {
    if(c2==0)
      g.setColor(Color.blue);
    else
      g.setColor(Color.cyan);
    g.fillRect(x, y, n, n);
    recSquares(x + n, y, n/2, g);
 }
}
```

ANALYSIS	
BASIC OPERATION:	Drawing one pixel
PROBLEM SIZE:	n
RECURRENCE BASE CASE:	$T(1) = 0$
RECURRENCE RECURSIVE STEP:	$T(n) = T(n/2) + n^2$, for all n>1.

SOLVING RECURRENCE

$T(1) = 0$
$T(n) = T(n/2) + n^2$, for n>1.

Assume that n is 2^k.

$$
\begin{aligned}
T(n) &= T(n/2) + n^2 \\
&= (T(n/2^2) + (n/2)^2) + n^2 = T(n/2^2) + (n/2)^2 + n^2 \\
&= T(n/2^3) + (n/2^2)^2 + (n/2)^2 + n^2 \\
&\ \ \ldots \\
&= T(n/2^k) + (n/2^{k-1})^2 + \ldots + (n/2^2)^2 + (n/2)^2 + n^2 \\
&= T(1) + n^2/2^{2k-2}\,(1 + 2^2 + 2^4 + \ldots + 2^{2k-2}) \\
&= 0 + (4n^2/n^2)(1 + 2^2 + 2^4 + \ldots + 2^{2k-2}) \\
&= 4\sum_{i=0}^{k-1} 2^{2i} \\
&= 4\,\frac{4^k - 1}{3} \\
&= (4/3)(n^2 - 1)
\end{aligned}
$$

$T(n)$ is in $\Theta(n^2)$. Running time is quadratic function of n.

12) Given an array of size n whose elements are zeros and ones and all zero elements precede ones, this algorithm finds the number of the zero elements.

```
PRECONDITION: first>=0, last>=0, first<=last
int countZeros(int[] list, int first, int last)
{
 if ( first > last )
```

```
    return 0;
 else if ( first == last )
 {
    if ( list[first] == 0 )
      return 1;
    else
      return 0;
  }
  else
  {
    int mid = (first + last)/2;
    if ( list[mid] == 0 )
      return (mid - first + 1) + countZeros(list, mid+1, last);
    else
      return countZeros(list, first, mid-1);
  }
}
```

ANALYSIS	
BASIC OPERATION:	Comparing a list element with zero
PROBLEM SIZE:	n denoting last-first+1
RECURRENCE BASE CASE:	$T(1) = 1$,
RECURRENCE RECURSIVE STEP:	$T(n) = T(n/2) + 1$, for all $n>=1$.

SOLVING RECURRENCE

$T(1) = 1$,
$T(n) = T(n/2) + 1$, for all $n>1$.

Assume that $n = 2^k$, and so, $k = \lg n$.

$$
\begin{aligned}
T(2^k) &= T(2^{k-1}) + 1 = (\, T(2^{k-2}) + 1\,) + 1 \\
&= T(2^{k-2}) + 2 = (\, T(2^{k-3}) + 1\,) + 2 \\
&= T(2^{k-3}) + 3 \\
&\ \ \ldots \\
&= T(2^{k-k}) + k \\
&= T(1) + k \\
&= k + 1
\end{aligned}
$$

$T(n) = \lg n + 1$

$T(n)$ is in $\Theta(\lg n)$. Running time is logarithmic.

CHAPTER 3

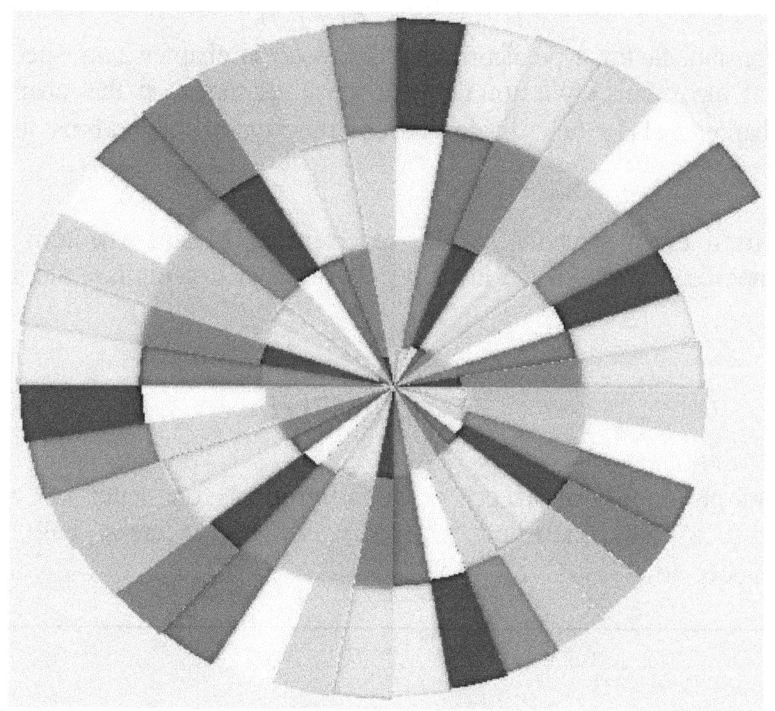

RUNNING TIME ANALYSIS OF DIVIDE-AND-CONQUER RECURSIVE ALGORITHMS

Recurrences type: $T(n) = aT(n/b) + f(n)$.
Constant a is positive integer, constant $b>1$, and function $f(n)$ is nonrecursive cost.

This chapter includes running time analysis of recursive algorithms of size n that invoke number a subproblems of size reduced by positive constant factor b. The recurrences are of type

$$T(n) = a\,T(n / b) + f(n).$$

Constant a is positive integer i.e. $a >= 1$. Constant b is also positive but is strictly greater than 1 i.e. $b>1$. Division operator n / b is integer division which returns the integer portion of the result (also called floor function). We will use the standard approach to perform an analysis by assuming that $n = b^k$ for some nonnegative integer k. As discussed in chapter 2 this does not limit the generality, and at the same time makes solving recurrences much simpler.

In special cases when $a = 1$, divide-and-conquer type problems have corresponding recurrences as follows:

$$T(n) = T(n / b) + f(n).$$

So, all reduce-by-constant-factor type algorithms discussed in chapter 2 are special cases of divide-and-conquer type of algorithms. We don't repeat those examples in this chapter. The examples presented in this chapter include only divide-and-conquer type of algorithms for which constant a is greater than one.

When we do not need exact solutions of the recurrences, Master Theorem can be applied to determine the asymptotic growth of the resulting $T(n)$ based just on the values of constants a, b, and d.

EXAMPLES

1) For a given positive integer n, algorithm prints one letter "A" when n is one, and otherwise, it prints one letter "A", and makes two recursive calls to subproblems of size reduced to $n/2$.

```
void letters (int n)
{
   if (n==1)
     System.out.println("A");
   else
   {
     System.out.println("A");
     letters(n/2);
     letters(n/2);
   }
}
```

ANALYSIS

BASIC OPERATION:	Print one letter "A"
PROBLEM SIZE:	n
RECURRENCE BASE CASE:	T(1) = 1
RECURRENCE RECURSIVE STEP:	T(n) = 2T(n/2) + 1

SOLVING RECURRENCES

$T(1) = 1$
$T(n) = 2T(n/2) + 1$, for $n>1$.

Assume that $n=2^k$ and consequently $k = \log_2 n$.

$= 2(2T(n/2^2) + 1) + 1 = 2^2T(n/2^2) + 2 + 1$
$= 2^2(2T(n/2^3) + 1) + 2 + 1 = 2^3T(n/2^3) + 2^2 + 2^1 + 2^0$
$= 2^3(2T(n/2^4) + 1) + 2^2 + 2^1 + 2^0 = 2^4T(n/2^4) + 2^3 + 2^2 + 2^1 + 2^0$
...
$= 2^kT(n/2^k) + 2^{k-1} + 2^{k-2} + \cdots + 2^2 + 2^1 + 2^0$
$= 2^kT(1) + 2^{k-1} + 2^{k-2} + \cdots + 2^2 + 2^1 + 2^0$
$= 2^k + 2^{k-1} + 2^{k-2} + \cdots + 2^2 + 2^1 + 2^0$
$= \sum_{i=0}^{k} 2^i$
$= 2^{k+1} - 1$
$= 2n - 1$

T(n) is in $\Theta(n)$. T(n) is linear.

2) Algorithm determines the sum of elements in a nonempty array *list*.

// First and last represent the index of the first and last subarray element, respectively.

```
int arrSum(int list[], int first, int last)
{
   if(first == last)
     return list[first];
   else
     return arrSum(list, first, (first+last)/2) +
            arrSum(list, (first+last)/2 + 1, last);
}
```

ANALYSIS

BASIC OPERATION:	+
PROBLEM SIZE:	n denoting last - first + 1 (or list size) .
RECURRENCE BASE CASE:	T(1) = 0
RECURRENCE RECURSIVE STEP:	T(n) = 2T(n/2) + 1

SOLVING RECURRENCES

T(1) = 0

T(n) = 2T(n/2) + 1, for n>1. Assume that $n=2^k$ and consequently $k = \log_2 n$.

$= 2(2T(n/2^2) + 1) + 1 = 2^2T(n/2^2) + 2 + 1$

$= 2^2(2T(n/2^3) + 1) + 2 + 1 = 2^3T(n/2^3) + 2^2 + 2^1 + 2^0$

$= 2^3(2T(n/2^4) + 1) + 2^2 + 2^1 + 2^0 = 2^4T(n/2^4) + 2^3 + 2^2 + 2^1 + 2^0$

...

$= 2^kT(n/2^k) + 2^{k-1} + 2^{k-2} + \text{- - -} + 2^2 + 2^1 + 2^0$

$= 2^kT(1) + 2^{k-1} + 2^{k-2} + \text{- - -} + 2^2 + 2^1 + 2^0$

$= 2^{k-1} + 2^{k-2} + \text{- - -} + 2^2 + 2^1 + 2^0$

$= \sum_{i=0}^{k-1} 2^i$

$= 2^k - 1$

$= n - 1$

T(n) is in Θ(n). T(n) is linear.

3) Algorithm computes a power of a real number d raised to a positive integer n. The following definitions are used: If $n=1$, $d^n = d$. Otherwise, if n is positive and even, $d^n = d^{n/2} * d^{n/2}$. and if n is positive and odd, $d^n = d * d^{n/2} * d^{n/2}$. Do the best case performance analysis when $n = 2^k$ for k a positive integer. Note that $n \% 2$ is always 0 in such case. Only two subproblems are called. Both subproblems reduce the size by half. In addition, one basic operation is performed.

```
// Precondition: n positive integer
double power2(double d, int n)
 {
    if (n == 0)
      return 1;
    if (n == 1)
      return d;
    else if (n % 2 == 0)
      return power2(d, n/2)* power2(d, n/2);
```

```
    else
      return d * power2(d, n/2)* power2(d, n/2);
}
```

ANALYSIS	**Best case performance**
BASIC OPERATION:	*
PROBLEM SIZE:	n
RECURRENCE BASE CASE:	T(0) = 0, T(1) = 0
RECURRENCE RECURSIVE STEP:	T(n) = 2T(n/2) + 1

SOLVING RECURRENCES

T(0) = 0, T(1) = 0

T(n) = 2T(n/2) + 1, for n>1. Assume that $n=2^k$ and consequently $k = \log_2 n$.

$= 2(2T(n/2^2) + 1) + 1 = 2^2T(n/2^2) + 2 + 1$

$= 2^2(2T(n/2^3) + 1) + 2 + 1 = 2^3T(n/2^3) + 2^2 + 2^1 + 2^0$

$= 2^3(2T(n/2^4) + 1) + 2^2 + 2^1 + 2^0 = 2^4T(n/2^4) + 2^3 + 2^2 + 2^1 + 2^0$

...

$= 2^kT(n/2^k) + 2^{k-1} + 2^{k-2} + \ldots + 2^2 + 2^1 + 2^0$

$= 2^kT(1) + 2^{k-1} + 2^{k-2} + \ldots + 2^2 + 2^1 + 2^0$

$= 2^{k-1} + 2^{k-2} + \ldots + 2^2 + 2^1 + 2^0$

$= \sum_{i=0}^{k-1} 2^i$

$= 2^k - 1$

$= n - 1$

T(n) is in Θ(n). T(n) is linear.

3) Algorithm performs merge sort for list of n elements. List can be empty or not.

```
void mergeSort(int[] list, int n)
{
    if(n > 1)
    {
       int[] list1 = new int[n/2], list2 = new int[n-n/2];
```

```
        int n1,n2,k;
        for(n1 = 0; n1 < n/2; n1++)
          list1[n1] = list[n1];
        for(k = n/2, n2=0; k < n; k++,n2++)
          list2[n2] = list[k];
        mergeSort(list1,n1);
        mergeSort(list2,n2);
        merge(list, n, list1, n1, list2, n2);
    }
}

void merge(int[] list, int n, int[] list1, int n1, int[] list2,
           int n2)
{
    int i1 = 0, i2 = 0;
    while(i1 < n1 && i2 < n2)
    {
      if(list1[i1] < list2[i2])
      {
        list[i1 + i2] = list1[i1];
        i1++;
      }
      else
      {
        list[i1 + i2] = list2[i2];
        i2++;
      }
    }
    if(i1 == n1)
      for(;i2 < n2;i2++)
          list[i1 + i2] = list2[i2];
    else
      for(;i1 < n1;i1++)
          list[i1 + i2] = list1[i1];
}
```

ANALYSIS	
BASIC OPERATION:	Comparison of list elements
PROBLEM SIZE:	n
RECURRENCE BASE CASES:	$T(0) = 0$, $T(1) = 0$
RECURRENCE RECURSIVE STEP:	$T(n) = 2T(n/2) + n - 1$, for $n>1$

SOLVING RECURRENCES

$T(0) = 0, T(1) = 0$

$T(n) = 2T(n/2) + n-1$, for $n>1$. Assume that $n=2^k$ and consequently $k = \log_2 n$.

$= 2T(2^{k-1}) + 2^k - 1$

$= 2(2T(2^{k-2}) + 2^{k-1} - 1) + 2^k - 1 = 2^2T(2^{k-2}) + 2^k - 2 + 2^k - 1 = 2^2T(2^{k-2}) + 2\ 2^k - (2^1 + 2^0)$

$= 2^2(2T(2^{k-3}) + 2^{k-2} - 1) + 2\ 2^k - (2^1 + 2^0) = 2^3T(2^{k-3}) + 3\ 2^k - (2^2 + 2^1 + 2^0)$

...

$= 2^kT(2^{k-k}) + k\ 2^k - (2^{k-1} + \ldots + 2^2 + 2^1 + 2^0)$

$= 2^k\, T(1) + k\ 2^k - \sum_{i=0}^{k-1} 2^i$

$= 0 + n \lg n - (2^k - 1)$

$= n \lg n - n + 1$

$T(n)$ is in $\Theta(n \log n)$.

5) Algorithm draws C-curve. Basic operation is drawing one pixel on a graphical surface.

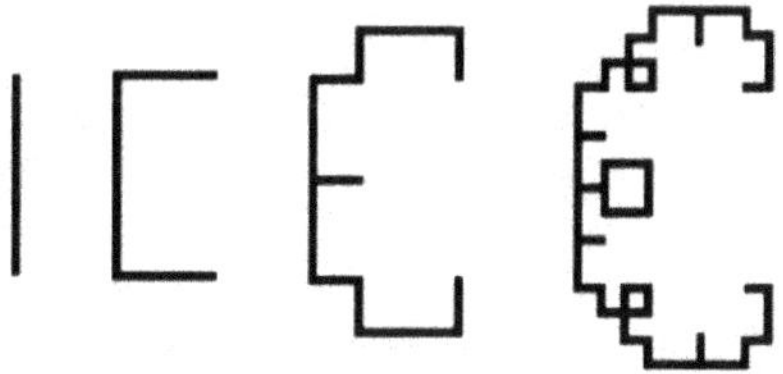

Problem size is n which is also the length of the starting vertical line. The line is not drawn. Direction in general can be either down, right, left, or up ("D", "R","L", or "U"). There are only four recursive calls, each with n reduced by half, and no non-recursive cost. If n is 1, one pixel is drawn as a line from point x,y to x,y. The first four steps to follow for lines that are not drawn are as follows:

```
public void recC (int x, int y, int n, String dir, Graphics g)
{
  if (n <= 1)
    g.drawLine(x,y, x,y);
  else if (dir.equals("D"))
  {
    recC(x,y, n/2,"L",g);
    recC(x-n/2,y,n/2,"D",g);
    recC(x-n/2,y+n/2,n/2,"D",g);
    recC(x-n/2,y+n,n/2,"R",g);
  }
  else if (dir.equals("R"))
  {
    recC(x,y,n/2,"D",g);
    recC(x,y+n/2,n/2,"R",g);
    recC(x+n/2,y+n/2,n/2,"R",g);
    recC(x+n,y+n/2,n/2,"U",g);
  }
  else if (dir.equals("L"))
  {
    recC(x,y,n/2,"U",g);
    recC(x,y-n/2,n/2,"L",g);
    recC(x-n/2,y-n/2,n/2,"L",g);
    recC(x-n,y-n/2,n/2,"D",g);
  }
  else if (dir.equals("U"))
  {
    recC(x,y, n/2,"R",g);
    recC(x+n/2,y, n/2,"U",g);
    recC(x+n/2,y-n/2, n/2,"U",g);
    recC(x+n/2,y-n, n/2,"L",g);
  }
}
```

ANALYSIS

BASIC OPERATION:	Drawing one pixel
PROBLEM SIZE:	n
RECURRENCE BASE CASE:	$T(1) = 1$
RECURRENCE RECURSIVE STEP:	$T(n) = 4T(n/2)$

SOLVING RECURRENCES

$T(1) = 1$
$T(n) = 4T(n/2)$ Assume that $n=2^k$
$= 4^2T(n/2^2)$
$= 4^3T(n/2^3)$
. . .
$= 4^kT(n/2^k)$
$= (2^k)^2 T(1)$
$= n^2$

$T(n)$ is in $\Theta(n^2)$. $T(n)$ is quadratic.

6) Algorithm draws squares as shown. Use Master theorem to determine only the asymptotic growth of *T(n)*.

At the highest level of recursion the outline of the largest square centered in the center of the applet is drawn. In addition, four recursive calls are made. Each of the four subproblems has *x, y* equal to one of the corners of the largest square. The subproblems have size reduced from *n* to *n*/2. Base case is when *n* is less than or equal to 16. Nothing is done in such case.

Auxiliary method `square` is used instead of Java method `drawRect` which uses x,y for upper left corner of the rectangle. Method `square` draws the outline of a square centered in *x,y* and side length equal to *n*.

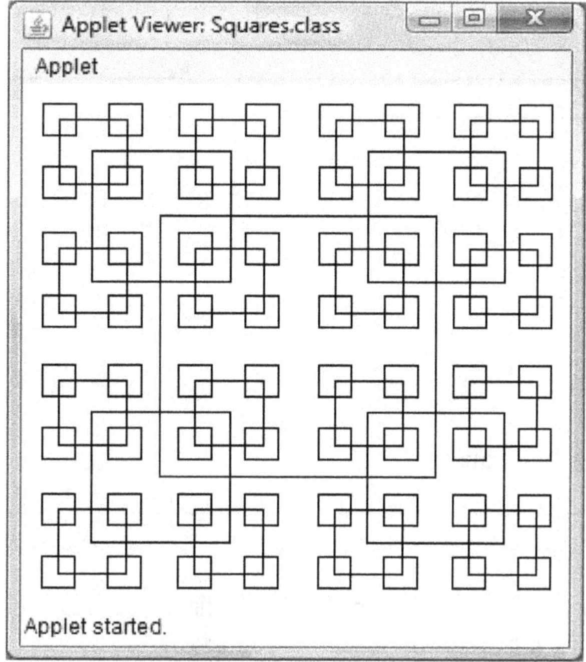

```
// draw a square with side equal to n and centered at x,y.
 private void square(int x, int y, int n, Graphics g)
 {
   g.drawRect(x-n/2, y-n/2, n, n);
 }

 public void recSquares(int x, int y, int n, Graphics g)
 {
   if ( n > 16)
   {
     recSquares(x-n/2, y+n/2, n/2, g);
     recSquares(x+n/2, y+n/2, n/2, g);
     recSquares(x+n/2, y-n/2, n/2, g);
     recSquares(x-n/2, y-n/2, n/2, g);
     square(x, y, n, g);
   }
 }
```

ANALYSIS

BASIC OPERATION:	Drawing one pixel
PROBLEM SIZE:	n
RECURRENCE BASE CASE:	T(i) = 0 for i <= 16
RECURRENCE RECURSIVE STEP:	T(n) = 4T(n/2) + 4n

SOLVING RECURRENCES

T(i) = 0, for i<=16
T(n) = 4T(n/2) + 4n, for n>16.

Master theorem applied: a=4, b=2, d=1
Since $a>b^d$ it follows that T(n) is in $\Theta(n^{\log_b a})$. So T(n) is in $\Theta(n^{\log_2 4})$.

T(n) is in $\Theta(n^2)$. T(n) is quadratic.

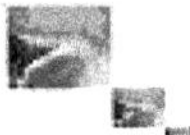

7) Algorithm draws squares as shown. This time squares are filled with color. We use alternating colors for different levels of recursion.

At the highest level of recursion the largest square is drawn and it is centered in the center of the applet. The largest square has size n x n. Before drawing that largest square, four recursive calls are made to four subproblems each one centered in one of the corners of the square. All four subproblems have size reduced from n to n/2.

Base case is when n is equal to 1. Nothing is done in such a case. Problem size is input parameter n used to draw the largest square of size n x n. Basic operation is drawing one pixel. The nonrecursive cost at the highest level is filling the square with current color, which is n^2. The cost of four recursive calls is $4T(n/2)$.

Verify asymptotic growth for resulting T(n) by using Master Theorem.

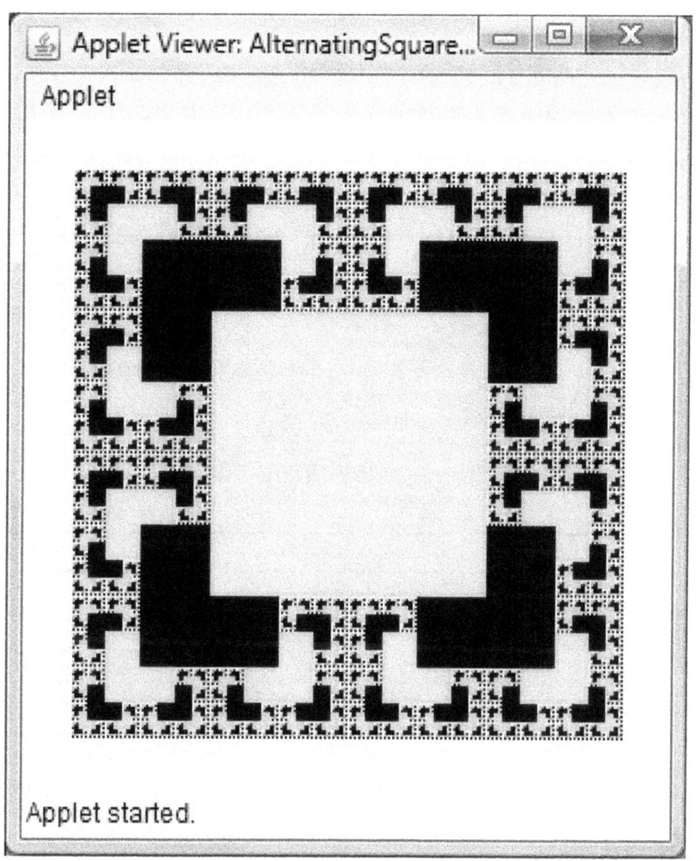


```
//Auxiliary method to draw square centered at x,y with side length equal to n
private void square(int x, int y, int n, Graphics g)
{
  g.fillRect(x-n/2, y-n/2, n, n);
}

public void recSquare(int x, int y, int n, Graphics g, int k)
```

```
{
  if (n == 1)
    square(x, y, 1, g);
  else if ( n > 1 )
  {
      recSquare(x-n/2, y+n/2, n/2, g, k+1);
      recSquare(x+n/2, y+n/2, n/2, g, k+1);
      recSquare(x+n/2, y-n/2, n/2, g, k+1);
      recSquare(x-n/2, y-n/2, n/2, g, k+1);
      if ( k%2 == 0 )
        g.setColor(Color.cyan);
      else
        g.setColor(Color.black);
      square(x, y, n, g);
  }
}
```

ANALYSIS

BASIC OPERATION:	Drawing one pixel
PROBLEM SIZE:	n
RECURRENCE BASE CASE:	$T(1) = 1$
RECURRENCE RECURSIVE STEP:	$T(n) = 4T(n/2) + n^2$

SOLVING RECURRENCES

$T(1) = 1$
$T(n) = 4T(n/2) + n^2$

Let assume that n is a power of two. Since, $n=2^k$, $k = \lg n$.

$= 4T(2^{k-1}) + 2^{2k}$
$= 4(4T(2^{k-2}) + 2^{2(k-1)}) + 2^{2k}$
$= 4^2T(2^{k-2}) + 4*2^{2(k-1)} + 2^{2k}$
$= 4^2T(2^{k-2}) + 2*2^{2k}$
$= 4^2 (4T(2^{k-3}) + 2^{2(k-2)}) + 2*2^{2k}$
$= 4^3T(2^{k-3}) + 3*2^{2k}$
...
$= 4^kT(2^{k-k}) + k*2^{2k}$
$= n^2\ T(1) + n^2 \lg n = n^2 \lg n + n^2$

$T(n) = n^2 \lg n + n^2$. T(n) has asymptotic growth: $\Theta(n^2 \lg n)$

It is easy to verify asymptotic growth by applying Master Theorem : $a = 4$, $b = 2$, and $d = 2$.

Since $a = b^d$, $T(n)$ is in $\Theta(n^2 \lg n)$.

8) Algorithm draws Sierpinski triangles as shown.

At highest level of recursion the largest triangle is drawn. Assume that problem size n is the length of triangle sides next to the right angle. Non-recursive cost is drawing two sides of legth n and drawing hypotenuse of length $n\sqrt{2}$ which is $2n + n\sqrt{2}$. In addition to drawing the three sides of a triangle, three recursive subproblems are invoked. One uses x,y of the top corner of the original triangle and the other two are using two midpoints on the two adjacent sides of that corner point. The size of each subproblem is reduced by half.

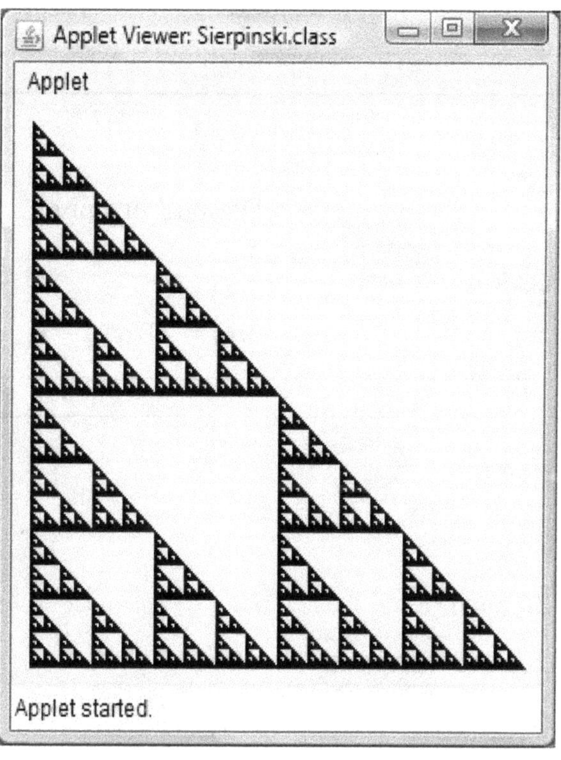


```
private final int SIZE = 300;
private final int DIST = 10;
public void recTriangles(int x, int y, int n, Graphics g)
{
    int x1 = x;
    int y1 = y;
```

```
    int x2 = x;
    int y2 = y + n - 1;
    int x3 = x + n - 1;
    int y3 = y + n - 1;
    if (n == 1 )
       g.drawLine(x, y, x, y);
    else if (n > 1)
    {
      g.drawLine(x1,y1,x2,y2);
      g.drawLine(x2,y2,x3,y3);
      g.drawLine(x3,y3,x1,y1);
      recTriangles(x1, y1, n/2, g);
      recTriangles((x1+x2)/2, (y1+y2)/2, n/2, g);
      recTriangles((x1+x3)/2, (y1+y3)/2, n/2, g);
    }
}
```

ANALYSIS

BASIC OPERATION:	Drawing one pixel
PROBLEM SIZE:	n
RECURRENCE BASE CASE:	$T(1) = 1$
RECURRENCE RECURSIVE STEP:	$T(n) = 3T(n/2) + n(2+\sqrt{2})$

SOLVING RECURRENCES

$T(1) = 1$

$T(n) = 3T(n/2) + n(2+\sqrt{2})$, for $n>1$.

Assume that $n = 2^k$, and consequently $k = \lg n$.

$$= 3T(2^{k-1}) + 2^k(2+\sqrt{2})$$
$$= 3(3T(2^{k-2}) + 2^{k-1}(2+\sqrt{2})) + 2^k(2+\sqrt{2})$$
$$= 3^2 T(2^{k-2}) + 3 * 2^{k-1}(2+\sqrt{2}) + 2^k(2+\sqrt{2})$$
$$= 3^2(3T(2^{k-3}) + 2^{k-2}(2+\sqrt{2})) + 3 * 2^{k-1}(2+\sqrt{2}) + 2^k(2+\sqrt{2})$$
$$= 3^3 T(2^{k-3}) + 3^2 * 2^{k-2}(2+\sqrt{2}) + 3 * 2^{k-1}(2+\sqrt{2}) + 2^k(2+\sqrt{2})$$
$$\ldots$$
$$= 3^k T(2^{k-k}) + 3^{k-1} * 2^{k-(k-1)}(2+\sqrt{2}) + \ldots + 3 * 2^{k-1}(2+\sqrt{2}) + 2^k(2+\sqrt{2})$$
$$= 3^k T(1) + (2+\sqrt{2}) * (3^{k-1} * 2^1 + 3^{k-2} * 2^2 + \ldots 3^1 * 2^{k-1} + 3^0 * 2^k)$$

$= 3^k + (2+\sqrt{2}) * 2^k * ((3/2)^{k-1} + (3/2)^{k-2} + \ldots + (3/2)^1 + (3/2)^0)$

$= 3^{\lg n} + (2+\sqrt{2})\ n * \frac{(\frac{3}{2})^k - 1)}{\frac{3}{2} - 1}$

$= n^{\lg 3} + (2+\sqrt{2})\ n * 2*((\frac{3}{2})^k - 1)$

$= n^{\lg 3} + (2+\sqrt{2})\ n * 2*(3^{\lg n}/n - 1)$

$= n^{\lg 3} + 2\,(2+\sqrt{2})\ n^{\lg 3} - 2\,(2+\sqrt{2})\ n$

$= (1 + 2\,(2+\sqrt{2})\ )\, n^{\lg 3} - 2\,(2+\sqrt{2})\ n$

Asymptotic performance: T(n) is in $\Theta(n^{\lg 3})$.

We can verify asymptotic performance by applying Master theorem:
a=3, b= 2 , d=1.
Since $a > b^d$, it follows that T(n) is in $\Theta(n^{\lg 3})$.
T(n) is between linear and quadratic.

9) Algorithm draws Sierpinski triangles as shown.

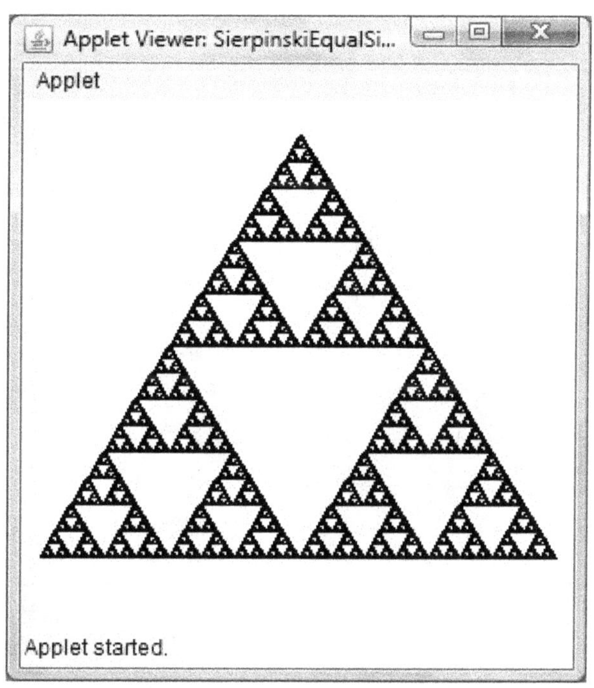

The difference from example 8) is that now all three sides have the same length n. At the highest level it draws three lines to connect three points that make an equilateral triangle. In addition, three recursive calls are made with six parameters that correspond to the x,y coordinates of the three smaller triangles, and graphics parameter that specifies the drawing surface. The size of each subproblem is reduced by half. Three pairs of x,y coordinates in three subproblems represent one of the corners of the current triangle with two midpoints on the two sides coming from the corner.

Stopping case is when the length of the triangle side is below given limit.

```
private final int SIZE = 300;
private final int DIST = 10;

public void recT (int x1, int y1, int x2, int y2, int x3,
                          int y3, Graphics g)
{
   if ( (x1-x2)*(x1-x2) + (y1-y2)*(y1-y2) == 1 )
      g.drawLine(x1,y1,x2,y2);
   else if ( (x1-x2)*(x1-x2) + (y1-y2)*(y1-y2) > 1 )
   {
     g.drawLine(x1,y1,x2,y2);
     g.drawLine(x2,y2,x3,y3);
     g.drawLine(x3,y3,x1,y1);
     recT ((x1+x2)/2,(y1+y2)/2,(x1+x3)/2,(y1+y3)/2, x1,y1,g);
     recT ((x1+x2)/2,(y1+y2)/2,(x3+x2)/2,(y3+y2)/2, x2,y2,g);
     recT ((x1+x3)/2,(y1+y3)/2,(x3+x2)/2,(y3+y2)/2, x3,y3,g);
   }
 }
```

ANALYSIS

BASIC OPERATION:	Drawing one pixel
PROBLEM SIZE:	n (distance between x1,y1 and x2,y2.)
RECURRENCE BASE CASE:	$T(1) = 3$
RECURRENCE RECURSIVE STEP:	$T(n) = 3T(n/2) + 3n$

SOLVING RECURRENCES

$T(0) = 0,\ T(1) = 3$

$T(n) = 3T(n/2) + 3n$, let $n=2^k$.

$$T(2^k) = 3T(2^{k-1}) + 3*2^k$$

$$= 3(3T(2^{k-2}) + 3*2^{k-1}) + 3*2^k = 3^2\, T(2^{k-2}) + 3^2*2^{k-1} + 3*2^k$$

$$= 3^2\,(3T(2^{k-3}) + 3*2^{k-2}) + 3^2*2^{k-1} + 3*2^k = 3^3\, T(2^{k-3}) + 3^3*2^{k-2} + 3^2*2^{k-1} + 3*2^k$$

$$= 3^3(3\, T(2^{k-4}) + 3*2^{k-3}) + 3^3*2^{k-2} + 3^2*2^{k-1} + 3*2^k$$

$$= 3^4\, T(2^{k-4}) + 3^4*2^{k-3} + 3^3*2^{k-2} + 3^2*2^{k-1} + 3*2^k$$

$$= 3^i\, T(2^{k-i}) + 3^i*2^{k-(i-1)} + \ldots + 3^3*2^{k-2} + 3^2*2^{k-1} + 3*2^k$$

$= 3^k T(2^{k-k}) + 3^k * 2^{k-(k-1)} + \ldots + 3^3 * 2^{k-2} + 3^2 * 2^{k-1} + 3 * 2^k$

$= 3^k T(1) + 3^k * 2^1 + 3^{k-1} * 2^2 + \ldots + 3^3 * 2^{k-2} + 3^2 * 2^{k-1} + 3 * 2^k$

$= 3^{k+1} + 3^k * 2^1 + 3^{k-1} * 2^2 + \ldots + 3^3 * 2^{k-2} + 3^2 * 2^{k-1} + 3 * 2^k$

$= 3^{k+1} (1 + (2/3)^1 + (2/3)^2 + \ldots + (2/3)^{k-2} + (2/3)^{k-1} + (2/3)^k)$

$= 3 * 3^k \sum_{i=0}^{k} (2/3)^i = 3 * 3^k \frac{\left(\frac{2}{3}\right)^{k+1} - 1}{\frac{2}{3} - 1} = 3 * 3^k \frac{1 - \left(\frac{2}{3}\right)^{k+1}}{\frac{1}{3}} = 3^2 * 3^k - 3 * 2^{k+1}$

Since $n = 2^k$, $k = \lg n$.

Further $3^k = 3^{\lg n} = 3^\wedge((\log_3 n)/(\log_3 2)) = n^{\lg 3}$. So, solution is

$T(n) = 9\ n^{\lg 3} - 6\ n.$

Since $\lg 2 < \lg 3 < \lg 4$ it follows that $1 < \lg 3 < 2$. Term n asymptotically grows slower than $n^{\lg 3}$ and can be ignored.

T(n) is in $\Theta(n^{\lg 3})$. T(n) is between linear and quadratic.

10) Algorithm draws squares as shown.

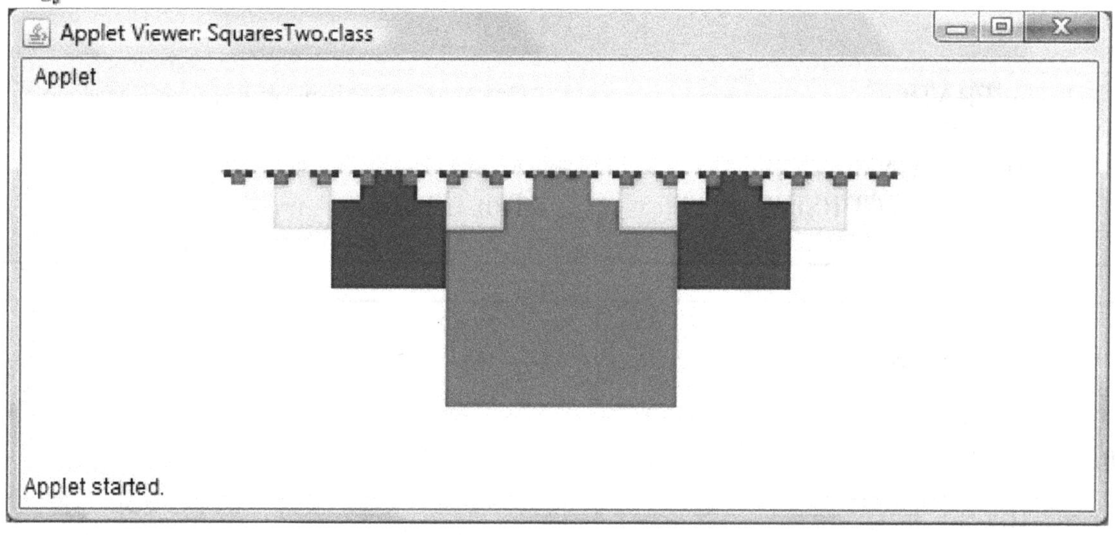

At the highest level of recursion the square with its upper left corner at x,y, and size n x n is drawn with the specified color. In addition, two recursive calls are made each reducing parameter n to n/2. For the first subproblem the new upper left corner is n/2 to the left of the largest square's upper left corner. For the second subproblem the new upper right corner is n/2 to the right of the largest square's upper right corner (which is n to the right from the left upper corner of the largest square).

```
private final int WIDTH = 600;
private final int HEIGHT = 200;
public void recSquares(int x, int y, int n, int color, Graphics g)
{
    if ( n > 1)
    {
      if(color%4==0)
       g.setColor(Color.red);
      else if (color%4==1)
       g.setColor(Color.blue);
      else if (color%4==2)
       g.setColor(Color.cyan);
      else
       g.setColor(Color.yellow);

      g.fillRect(x, y, n, n);
      recSquares(x-n/2, y, n/2, color+1, g);
      recSquares(x+n, y, n/2, color+1, g);
    }
}
```

ANALYSIS

BASIC OPERATION:	Drawing one pixel on graphical surface
PROBLEM SIZE:	n
RECURRENCE BASE CASE:	$T(1) = 0$
RECURRENCE RECURSIVE STEP:	$T(n) = 2\ T(n/2) + n^2$

SOLVING RECURRENCES

$T(1) = 0$
$T(n) = 2\ T(n/2) + n^2$, for $n>1$.

$$
\begin{aligned}
T(n) &= 2\ T(n/2) + n^2 \\
&= 2\ (2\ T(n/4) + (n/2)^2\ ) + n^2 \\
&= 2^2\ T(n/2^2) + n^2/2 + n^2 \\
&= 2^2\ (2\ T(n/2^3) + (n/2^2)^2\ ) + n^2/2 + n^2 \\
&= 2^3\ T(n/2^3) + n^2/2^2 + n^2/2 + n^2 \\
&\ldots
\end{aligned}
$$

$= 2^k T(n/2^k) + n^2/2^{k-1} + \ldots + n^2/2^1 + n^2/2^0$

Let $n=2^k$, and consequently $k = \lg n$.

$= n * 0 + n^2/2^k (\sum_{i=1}^{k} 2^i) = n (\sum_{i=0}^{k} 2^i - 1)$

$= n (\frac{2^{k+1}-1}{2-1} -1) = n (2n -2)$

$= 2 n^2 - 2 n$

T(n) is in $\Theta(n^2)$. T(n) is quadratic.

ANALYSIS

BASIC OPERATION:	*
PROBLEM SIZE:	n
RECURRENCE BASE CASE:	T(1) = 1
RECURRENCE RECURSIVE STEP:	T(n) = 3T(n/2)

SOLVING RECURRENCES

T(1) = 1

T(n) = 3T(n/2), for n>1. Assume that $n=2^k$, and consequently $k = \log_2 n$.

$= 3T(2^{k-1})$

$= 3^2T(2^{k-2})$

$= 3^3T(2^{k-3})$

. . .

$= 3^kT(2^{k-k})$

$= 3^k T(1)$

$= 3^k$

$= 3^{\log_2 n}$

$= n^{\log_2 3}$

$= n^{\lg 3}$

T(n) is in $\Theta(n^{\lg 3})$. T(n) is between linear and quadratic.

11) Algorithm performs Strassen matrix multiplication of two n x n matrices. Assume that $n=2^k$.

```
int[][] multiply(int[][] A, int[][] B)
{
  int n = A.length;
  int[][] R = new int[n][n];
  if (n == 1)
     R[0][0] = A[0][0] * B[0][0];
  else
  {
     int[][] A11 = new int[n/2][n/2];
     int[][] A12 = new int[n/2][n/2];
     int[][] A21 = new int[n/2][n/2];
     int[][] A22 = new int[n/2][n/2];
     int[][] B11 = new int[n/2][n/2];
     int[][] B12 = new int[n/2][n/2];
     int[][] B21 = new int[n/2][n/2];
     int[][] B22 = new int[n/2][n/2];
     split(A, A11, 0, 0);
     split(A, A12, 0, n/2);
     split(A, A21, n/2, 0);
     split(A, A22, n/2, n/2);
     split(B, B11, 0, 0);
     split(B, B12, 0, n/2);
     split(B, B21, n/2, 0);
     split(B, B22, n/2, n/2);
     int [][] M1 = multiply(add(A11, A22), add(B11, B22));
     int [][] M2 = multiply(add(A21, A22), B11);
     int [][] M3 = multiply(A11, sub(B12, B22));
     int [][] M4 = multiply(A22, sub(B21, B11));
     int [][] M5 = multiply(add(A11, A12), B22);
     int [][] M6 = multiply(sub(A21, A11), add(B11, B12));
     int [][] M7 = multiply(sub(A12, A22), add(B21, B22));
     int [][] C11 = add(sub(add(M1, M4), M5), M7);
     int [][] C12 = add(M3, M5);
     int [][] C21 = add(M2, M4);
     int [][] C22 = add(sub(add(M1, M3), M2), M6);
     join(C11, R, 0, 0);
     join(C12, R, 0, n/2);
     join(C21, R, n/2, 0);
     join(C22, R, n/2, n/2);
  }
  return R;
}
```

```
int[][] sub(int[][] A, int[][] B)
{
   int n = A.length;
   int[][] C = new int[n][n];
   for (int i = 0; i < n; i++)
     for (int j = 0; j < n; j++)
       C[i][j] = A[i][j] - B[i][j];
   return C;
}

int[][] add(int[][] A, int[][] B)
{
   int n = A.length;
   int[][] C = new int[n][n];
   for (int i = 0; i < n; i++)
      for (int j = 0; j < n; j++)
         C[i][j] = A[i][j] + B[i][j];
   return C;
}

void split(int[][] P, int[][] C, int iB, int jB)
{
   for(int i1 = 0, i2 = iB; i1 < C.length; i1++, i2++)
      for(int j1 = 0, j2 = jB; j1 < C.length; j1++, j2++)
         C[i1][j1] = P[i2][j2];
}

void join(int[][] C, int[][] P, int iB, int jB)
{
   for(int i1 = 0, i2 = iB; i1 < C.length; i1++, i2++)
      for(int j1 = 0, j2 = jB; j1 < C.length; j1++, j2++)
          P[i2][j2] = C[i1][j1];
}
```

ANALYSIS

BASIC OPERATION:	*
PROBLEM SIZE:	n
RECURRENCE BASE CASE:	$T(1) = 1$
RECURRENCE RECURSIVE STEP:	$T(n) = 7T(n/2)$

SOLVING RECURRENCES

$T(1) = 1$
$T(n) = 7T(n/2)$, for $n>1$.

Assume $n=2^k$ and consequently $k = \log_2 n$.

$= 7^2 T(n/2^2)$
$= 7^3 T(n/2^3)$
. . .
$= 7^k T(n/2^k)$
$= 7^k$
$= 7^{\log_2 n}$
$= 7^{\frac{\log 7\, n}{\log 7\, 2}}$
$= n^{\log_2 7}$
$= n^{\lg 7}$

$T(n)$ is in $\Theta(n^{\lg 7})$. Since $2 < \lg 7 < 3$, $T(n)$ is between quadratic and cubic.

CHAPTER 4

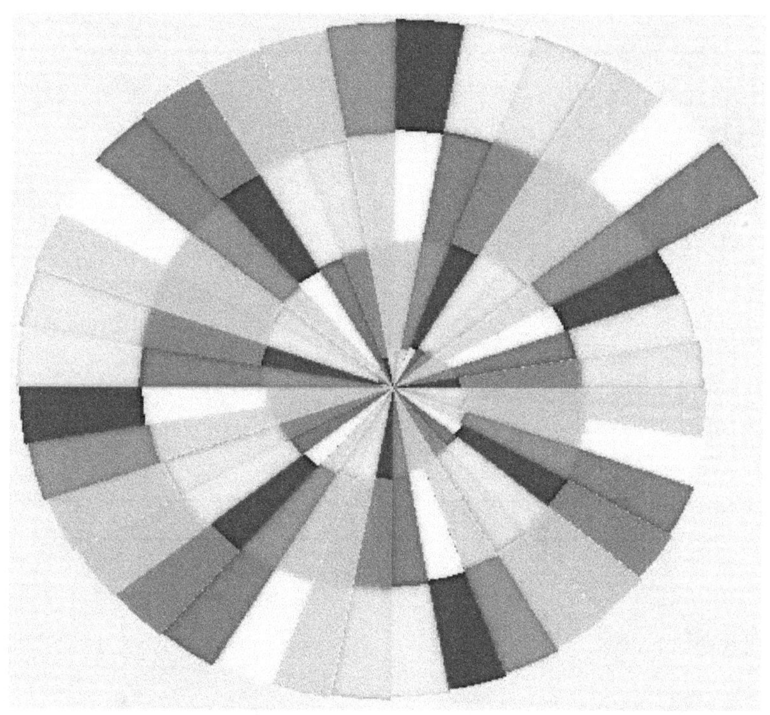

RUNNING TIME ANALYSIS OF GENERAL DECREASE RECURSIVE ALGORITHMS

Recurrences type: $T(n) = aT(n-1) + f(n)$, $aT(n) + bT(n-1) + cT(n-2) = f(n)$, and $T(n) = nT(n-1)$.

Constant a is not zero and function f(n) is nonrecursive cost.

This chapter includes examples of running time analyses that are generalizations of decrease by constant types. We cover several examples with second-order linear recurrences with constant coefficients. The recurrences are of type $a\,T(n) + b\,T(n-1) + c\,T(n-2) = f(n)$. If $f(n)$ is zero, the recurrence is a homogeneous second-order linear recurrence with constant coefficients. Constants a, b, and c are integers, and a is not zero. We start with the special case when $T(n) = 2\,T(n-1) + f(n)$, which means that $a = 1$, $b = -2$, $c = 0$, and then proceed to the general case. At the end we discuss algorithms of problem size n that invoke n subproblems on size n-1.

EXAMPLES

1) Algorithm prints letter "A" 2^{n-1} times. It does it by invoking two recursive subproblems of size n-1.

```
//PRECONDITION: n is positive
void printLetterExp(int n)
{
  if (n == 1)
    System.out.print ("A");
  else
  {
      printLetterExp(n-1);
      printLetterExp(n-1);
  }
}
```

ANALYSIS

BASIC OPERATION:	`System.out.print("A")`
PROBLEM SIZE:	n
RECURRENCE BASE CASE:	T(1) = 1
RECURRENCE RECURSIVE STEP:	T(n) = 2 T(n-1)

SOLVING RECURRENCES

$T(1) = 1$

$T(n) = 2T(n-1)$, for $n>1$.

$= 2\,(2\,T(n-2)\,) = 2^2\,T(n-2)$

$= 2^2\,(2\,T(n-3)\,) = 2^3\,T(n-3)$

. . .

$= 2^k T(n-k)$
Let k=n-1.
$= 2^{n-1} T(n-(n-1))$
$= 2^{n-1} T(1)$
$= 2^{n-1}$

T(n) is in $\Theta(2^n)$. T(n) is exponential.

2) Algorithm performs Tower of Hanoi puzzle.

```
//PRECONDITION: n is positive
void hanoi(int n, char from, char aux, char to)
{
  if (n == 1)
    System.out.print (from + " -> " + to);
  else
  {
      hanoi(n-1, from, to, aux);
      System.out.print (from + " -> " + to);
      hanoi(n-1, aux, from, to);
  }
}
```

ANALYSIS

BASIC OPERATION:	System.out.print for each disk move
PROBLEM SIZE:	n
RECURRENCE BASE CASE:	T(1) = 1
RECURRENCE RECURSIVE STEP:	T(n) = 2 T(n-1) + 1

SOLVING RECURRENCES

$T(1) = 1$
$T(n) = 2T(n-1) + 1$, for n>1.
$= 2(2T(n-2)+1) + 1 = 2^2 T(n-2) + 2 + 1$
$= 2^2(2T(n-3) + 1) = 2^3 T(n-3) + 2^2 + 2 + 1$
. . .
$= 2^k T(n-k) + 2^{k-1} + \ldots + 2^2 + 2 + 1$
$= 2^k T(n-k) + \sum_{i=0}^{k-1} 2^i$ Let k=n-1.

$= 2^k T(n-k) + 2^k - 1$

$= 2^{n-1} T(n-(n-1)) + 2^{n-1} - 1$

$= 2\, 2^{n-1} - 1$

$= 2^n - 1$

T(n) is in $\Theta(2^n)$. T(n) is exponential.

3) Algorithm calculates 2^n by using the following recursive definition. $2^n = 1$, if n equals 0, and $2^n = 2^{n-1} + 2^{n-1}$, if n is positive.

```
//PRECONDITION: n is nonnegative
int nThPowerOf2(int n)
{
  if (n == 0)
    return 1;
  else
  {
    return nThPowerOf2(n-1) + nThPowerOf2(n-1);
  }
}
```

ANALYSIS

BASIC OPERATION:	+
PROBLEM SIZE:	n
RECURRENCE BASE CASE:	T(0) = 0
RECURRENCE RECURSIVE STEP:	T(n) = 2 T(n-1) + 1

SOLVING RECURRENCES

$T(0) = 0$

$T(n) = 2T(n-1) + 1$, for n>1.

$= 2\,(2\,T(n-2)+1\,) + 1 = 2^2\,T(n-2) + 2 + 1$

$= 2^2\,(2\,T(n-3) + 1\,) = 2^3\,T(n-3) + 2^2 + 2 + 1$

. . .

$= 2^k\,T(n-k) + 2^{k-1} + \ldots + 2^2 + 2 + 1$

$= 2^k\,T(n-k) + \sum_{i=0}^{k-1} 2^i$ Let k=n.

$= 2^n\,T(n-n) + 2^n - 1$

$= 2^n T(0) + 2^n - 1$
$= 2^n - 1$

T(n) is in $\Theta(2^n)$. T(n) is exponential.

COMMENT: Obviously, the above is a very inefficient way of calculating 2 to the power of n. Using an equivalent equation $2^n = 2 * 2^{n-1}$ to implement the algorithm instead of $2^n = 2^{n-1} + 2^{n-1}$, would have been a significantly better choice. The corresponding algorithm to solve the same problem in that case would call only one subproblem of size n-1, and would have linear run time. See example 2 from chapter 1.

Finally, implementing the algorithm for the same problem by invoking only one subproblem of size n/2, would result in logarithmic time. See example 9 from chapter 2. That is, obviously, the most efficient of the three approaches.

We intentionally use inefficient algorithms in addition to the most efficient ones, in order to show that there could be a significant difference in time performance among various possible algorithms for solving the same problem. Examples of inefficient algorithms should improve learners skill and teach them to avoid less efficient code at design phase, before the implementation starts.

4) Algorithm determines n-th Fibonacci number for given nonnegative integer n.

```
//PRECONDITION: n≥0
int fibonacci(int n)
{
  if (n == 0)
    return 0;
  else if (n == 1)
    return 1;
  else if (n > 1)
    return fibonacci(n - 1) + fibonacci(n - 2)
}
```

ANALYSIS

BASIC OPERATION:	+
PROBLEM SIZE:	n
RECURRENCE BASE CASE:	T(0) = 0, T(1) = 0
RECURRENCE RECURSIVE STEP:	T(n) = T(n-1) + T(n-2) + 1

SOLVING RECURRENCES

$T(0) = 0, \quad T(1) = 0$
$T(n) = T(n-1) + T(n-2) + 1$, for $n>1$.

This is a second order linear inhomogeneous recurrence with constant coefficients. Recurrence $T(n) - T(n-1) - T(n-2) - 1 = 0$, can be transformed to $(T(n)+1) - (T(n-1)+1) - (T(n-2)+1) = 0$ by adding and subtracting 1.

After substitution $R(n) = T(n)+1$ the recurrence is transformed to the following second order linear homogeneous recurrence with constant coefficients: $R(0) = 1$, $R(1) = 1$, $R(n) - R(n-1) - R(n-2) = 0$, for $n>1$. The corresponding characteristic equation for that recurrence is $x^2 - x - 1 = 0$. The roots of this quadratic equation are $x_{1,2} = \frac{1\pm\sqrt{5}}{2}$.

The solution for the recurrence $R(n)$ is as follows: $R(n) = p\left(\frac{1+\sqrt{5}}{2}\right)^n + q\left(\frac{1-\sqrt{5}}{2}\right)^n$

Since, $R(0) = 1$, $R(1)=1$ should hold, constants p and q can be determined from the following two equations: $1 = p\left(\frac{1+\sqrt{5}}{2}\right)^0 + q\left(\frac{1-\sqrt{5}}{2}\right)^0$ and $1 = p\left(\frac{1+\sqrt{5}}{2}\right)^1 + q\left(\frac{1-\sqrt{5}}{2}\right)^1$. These are two linear equations with two unknown variables p, and q. The first one is $p+q = 1$. After substituting $q=1-p$ into the second equation we can calculate the values for p and q as follows: $p = \frac{1+\sqrt{5}}{2\sqrt{5}}$ and $q = -\frac{1-\sqrt{5}}{2\sqrt{5}}$.

So, the solution for recurrence $R(n)$ becomes: $R(n) = \frac{1}{\sqrt{5}}\left[\left(\frac{1+\sqrt{5}}{2}\right)^{n+1} - \left(\frac{1-\sqrt{5}}{2}\right)^{n+1}\right]$. Finally, since $T(n) = R(n) - 1$, the solution for $T(n)$ is: $T(n) = \frac{1}{\sqrt{5}}\left[\left(\frac{1+\sqrt{5}}{2}\right)^{n+1} - \left(\frac{1-\sqrt{5}}{2}\right)^{n+1}\right] - 1$.

Constant $\left(\frac{1-\sqrt{5}}{2}\right)$ is between -1 and 0. When n is very large $\left(\frac{1-\sqrt{5}}{2}\right)^n$ tends to zero. The value of the other constant $\left(\frac{1+\sqrt{5}}{2}\right) \approx 1.6$.

Consequently, $T(n)$ is in $\Theta\left(\left(\frac{1+\sqrt{5}}{2}\right)^n\right)$. $T(n)$ is exponential. $\frac{1+\sqrt{5}}{2}$ has approximate value 1.6.

5) Algorithm prints letter "A" one time if n is either 0 or 1. For n larger than 1, it invokes two recursive subproblems of size n-1 and size n-2, respectively.

```
//PRECONDITION: n is nonnegative
void printLetter(int n)
{
  if (n == 0) || (n == 1)
    System.out.print ("A");
  else if (n > 1)
  {
```

```
      printLetter (n-1);
      printLetter (n-2);
   }
}
```

ANALYSIS

BASIC OPERATION:	`System.out.print("A")`
PROBLEM SIZE:	n
RECURRENCE BASE CASE:	$T(0) = 1, \quad T(1) = 1$
RECURRENCE RECURSIVE STEP:	$T(n) = T(n-1) + T(n-2)$, for $n>1$.

SOLVING RECURRENCES

$T(0) = 1, \quad T(1) = 1$
$T(n) = T(n-1) + T(n-2)$, for $n>1$.

This is a second order linear homogeneous recurrence with constant coefficients. The corresponding characteristic equation is $x^2 - x - 1 = 0$. The roots of this quadratic equation are $x_{1,2} = \frac{1 \pm \sqrt{5}}{2}$

The solution for recurrence T(n) is as follows: $T(n) = p\left(\frac{1+\sqrt{5}}{2}\right)^n + q\left(\frac{1-\sqrt{5}}{2}\right)^n$.
Since T(0) =1, T(1)=1 should hold, constants p and q can be determined from the following two equations: $1 = p\left(\frac{1+\sqrt{5}}{2}\right)^0 + q\left(\frac{1-\sqrt{5}}{2}\right)^0$ and $1 = p\left(\frac{1+\sqrt{5}}{2}\right)^1 + q\left(\frac{1-\sqrt{5}}{2}\right)^1$.
These are two linear equations with two unknown variables p, and q. The first one is $p+q = 1$. After applying $q=1-p$ into the second equation we obtain the values for p and q.
$p = \frac{1+\sqrt{5}}{2\sqrt{5}}$ and $q = -\frac{1-\sqrt{5}}{2\sqrt{5}}$.
So, the solution for the recurrence T(n) becomes: $T(n) = \frac{1}{\sqrt{5}}\left[\left(\frac{1+\sqrt{5}}{2}\right)^{n+1} - \left(\frac{1-\sqrt{5}}{2}\right)^{n+1}\right]$.
Constant $\left(\frac{1-\sqrt{5}}{2}\right)$ is between -1 and 0. When n is very large $\left(\frac{1-\sqrt{5}}{2}\right)^n$ tends to zero. The value of the other constant $\left(\frac{1+\sqrt{5}}{2}\right) \approx 1.6$.

Consequently, T(n) is in $\Theta\left(\left(\frac{1+\sqrt{5}}{2}\right)^n\right)$. T(n) is exponential.

6) Algorithm is defined for nonnegative n. If n is 0 or 1 it does not do anything. If n is larger than 1 it prints letter "A" once, and it invokes two recursive subproblems of sizes n-1 and n-2, respectively.

```
//PRECONDITION: n is nonnegative
void printLetters(int n)
{
  if (n > 1)
  {
      System.out.print ("A");
      printLetters (n-1);
      printLetters (n-2);
  }
}
```

ANALYSIS

BASIC OPERATION:	`System.out.print ("A")`
PROBLEM SIZE:	n
RECURRENCE BASE CASE:	T(0) = 0, T(1) = 0
RECURRENCE RECURSIVE STEP:	T(n) = T(n-1) + T(n-2) + 1

SOLVING RECURRENCES

T(0) = 0, T(1) = 0
T(n) = T(n-1) + T(n-2) + 1, for n>1.

This is a second order nonhomogeneous recurrence with constant coefficients. T(n) - T(n-1) - T(n-2) – 1 = 0, can be transformed to (T(n)+1) - (T(n-1)+1) - (T(n-2)+1) = 0 by adding and subtracting 1. After substitution R(n) = T(n)+1 the recurrence is transformed to homogeneous: R(0) =1, R(1)=1, R(n) - R(n-1) - R(n-2) = 0, for n>1

The corresponding characteristic equation is $x^2 - x - 1 = 0$. The roots of this quadratic equation are $x_{1,2} = \frac{1\pm\sqrt{5}}{2}$. The solution for recurrence R(n) is: $R(n) = p\left(\frac{1+\sqrt{5}}{2}\right)^n + q\left(\frac{1-\sqrt{5}}{2}\right)^n$

Since R(0) =1, R(1)=1 should hold, constants p and q can be determined from the following two equations:

$1 = p\left(\frac{1+\sqrt{5}}{2}\right)^0 + q\left(\frac{1-\sqrt{5}}{2}\right)^0$ and $1 = p\left(\frac{1+\sqrt{5}}{2}\right)^1 + q\left(\frac{1-\sqrt{5}}{2}\right)^1$.

This are two linear equations with two unknown variables p, and q. The first one is p+q = 1. After substituting q=1-p, into second equation we calculate the values for p and q.

$p = \frac{1+\sqrt{5}}{2\sqrt{5}}$ and $q = -\frac{1-\sqrt{5}}{2\sqrt{5}}$.

So, the solution for recurrence R(n) becomes: $R(n) = \frac{1}{\sqrt{5}}\left[\left(\frac{1+\sqrt{5}}{2}\right)^{n+1} - \left(\frac{1-\sqrt{5}}{2}\right)^{n+1}\right]$.

Finally, since T(n) = R(n) - 1, the solution for T(n) is:
$T(n) = \frac{1}{\sqrt{5}}[(\frac{1+\sqrt{5}}{2})^{n+1} - (\frac{1-\sqrt{5}}{2})^{n+1}] - 1.$

Constant $\left(\frac{1-\sqrt{5}}{2}\right)$ is between -1 and 0. When n is very large $(\frac{1-\sqrt{5}}{2})^n$ tends to zero.
The value of the other constant $(\frac{1+\sqrt{5}}{2}) \approx 1.6.$

T(n) is in $\Theta((\frac{1+\sqrt{5}}{2})^n)$. T(n) is exponential.

7) Algorithm determines n-th Lucas number for given positive integer n.

```
//PRECONDITION: n>0
int lucas(int n)
{
  if (n == 1)
    return 1;
  else if (n == 2)
    return 3;
  else if (n > 2)
    return lucas(n - 1) + lucas(n - 2)
}
```

ANALYSIS

BASIC OPERATION:	+
PROBLEM SIZE:	n
RECURRENCE BASE CASE:	T(1) = 0, T(2) = 0
RECURRENCE RECURSIVE STEP:	T(n) = T(n-1) + T(n-2) + 1

SOLVING RECURRENCES

T(1) = 0, T(2) = 0
T(n) = T(n-1) + T(n-2) + 1, for n>1.

This is a second order nonhomogeneous recurrence with constant coefficients. Equation T(n) - T(n-1) - T(n-2) – 1 = 0, can be transformed to (T(n)+1) - (T(n-1)+1) - (T(n-2)+1) = 0 by adding and subtracting 1. After substitution R(n) = T(n)+1 the recurrence is transformed to homogeneous: R(1) =1, R(2)=1, R(n) - R(n-1) - R(n-2) = 0, for n>2. This is a second order linear homogeneous recurrence with constant coefficients. The corresponding characteristic equation is:

$x^2 - x - 1 = 0$. The roots of this quadratic equation are $x_{1,2} = \frac{1 \pm \sqrt{5}}{2}$

The solution for recurrence R(n) is as follows: $R(n) = p\left(\frac{1+\sqrt{5}}{2}\right)^n + q\left(\frac{1-\sqrt{5}}{2}\right)^n$

Since R(1) =1, R(2)=1 should hold, constants p and q can be determined from the following two equations:
$1 = p\left(\frac{1+\sqrt{5}}{2}\right)^1 + q\left(\frac{1-\sqrt{5}}{2}\right)^1$ and $1 = p\left(\frac{1+\sqrt{5}}{2}\right)^2 + q\left(\frac{1-\sqrt{5}}{2}\right)^2$. These are two linear equations with two unknown variables p, and q.

The values for p and q are: $p = \frac{1+\sqrt{5}}{5+\sqrt{5}}$ and $q = \frac{-1}{\sqrt{5}}$. So, the solution for recurrence R(n) becomes:
$R(n) = \frac{1+\sqrt{5}}{5+\sqrt{5}}\left(\frac{1+\sqrt{5}}{2}\right)^n - \frac{1}{\sqrt{5}}\left(\frac{1-\sqrt{5}}{2}\right)^n$. Finally, since T(n) = R(n) - 1, the solution for T(n) is:

$T(n) = \frac{1+\sqrt{5}}{5+\sqrt{5}}\left(\frac{1+\sqrt{5}}{2}\right)^n - \frac{1}{\sqrt{5}}\left(\frac{1-\sqrt{5}}{2}\right)^n - 1.$

Constant $\left(\frac{1-\sqrt{5}}{2}\right)$ is between -1 and 0. When n is very large $\left(\frac{1-\sqrt{5}}{2}\right)^n$ tends to zero. The value of the other constant $\left(\frac{1+\sqrt{5}}{2}\right) \approx 1.6$.

T(n) is in $\Theta\left(\left(\frac{1+\sqrt{5}}{2}\right)^n\right)$. T(n) is exponential.

8) Algorithm prints letter "A" factorial of *n* times. It does it by invoking *n* recursive subproblems of size *n*-1.

```
//PRECONDITION: n is positive
void printLetter(int n)
{
  if (n == 1)
    System.out.print ("A");
  else
  {
     for( int i=1; i<=n; i++)
      printLetter (n-1);
  }
}
```

ANALYSIS

BASIC OPERATION:	System.out.print ("A")
PROBLEM SIZE:	n

RECURRENCE BASE CASE:	$T(1) = 1$
RECURRENCE RECURSIVE STEP:	$T(n) = n * T(n-1)$

SOLVING RECURRENCES

$T(1) = 1$

$$
\begin{aligned}
T(n) &= n * T(n-1), \text{ for } n>1. \\
&= n * (n-1) * T(n-2) \\
&= n * (n-1) * (n-2) * T(n-3) \\
&\ldots \\
&= n * (n-1) * (n-2) * \ldots * 2 * T(n-(n-1)) \\
&= n * (n-1) * (n-2) * \ldots * 2 * 1 \\
&= n!
\end{aligned}
$$

$T(n)$ is in $\Theta(n!)$. This is much faster growing than exponential function.

9) Algorithm prints all permutations of n elements by using the interchanging approach introduced by mathematician B. Heap in 1963.

// PRECONDITION: n is positive.
// Array `list` is global variable.

```
static void heapPermute(int n)
{
   int temp;
   if (n == 1)
   {
      for(int i = 1; i <= N; i++)
         System.out.print(list[i]);
      System.out.println();
   }
   else
   {
     for(int i = 1; i <= n; i++)
     {
         heapPermute(n-1);
         if (n % 2 == 0)
         {
            temp = list[1];
            list[1] = list[n];
            list[n] = temp;
         }
```

```
        else
        {
           temp = list[i];
           list[i] = list[n];
           list[n] = temp;
        }
      }
   }
}
```

ANALYSIS

BASIC OPERATION:	%
PROBLEM SIZE:	n
RECURRENCE BASE CASE:	T(1) = 0
RECURRENCE RECURSIVE STEP:	T(n) = n * T(n-1) + n

SOLVING RECURRENCES

T(1) = 0

T(n) = n * T(n-1) + n
= n [(n-1) * T(n-2) + (n-1)] + n
= n(n-1) T(n-2) + n(n-1) + n
= n (n-1) * [(n-2) * T(n-3) +(n-2)] + n(n-1) + n
= n (n-1) (n-2) T(n-3) + n (n-1) (n-2) + n(n-1) + n
. . .
= n! * T(1) +n! + n (n-1) (n-2)…3 + n (n-1) (n-2)…4 + . . . + n(n-1) + n
= n! + n (n-1) (n-2)…3 + n (n-1) (n-2)…4 + . . . + n(n-1) + n
= n! [1 + 1/2! + 1/3! + 1/4! + …+ 1/(n-1)!]
$=n! * \sum_{i=1}^{n-1} \frac{1}{i!} < 2n!$

Since $k! > 2^k$, $1/k! < 1/2^k$. Since $\sum_{i=1}^{n-1} \frac{1}{2^i} < 2$, it follows that $\sum_{i=1}^{n-1} \frac{1}{i!} < 2$.

T(n) is in Θ(n!). T(n) is n! running time. T(n) grows faster than exponential function.

CHAPTER 5

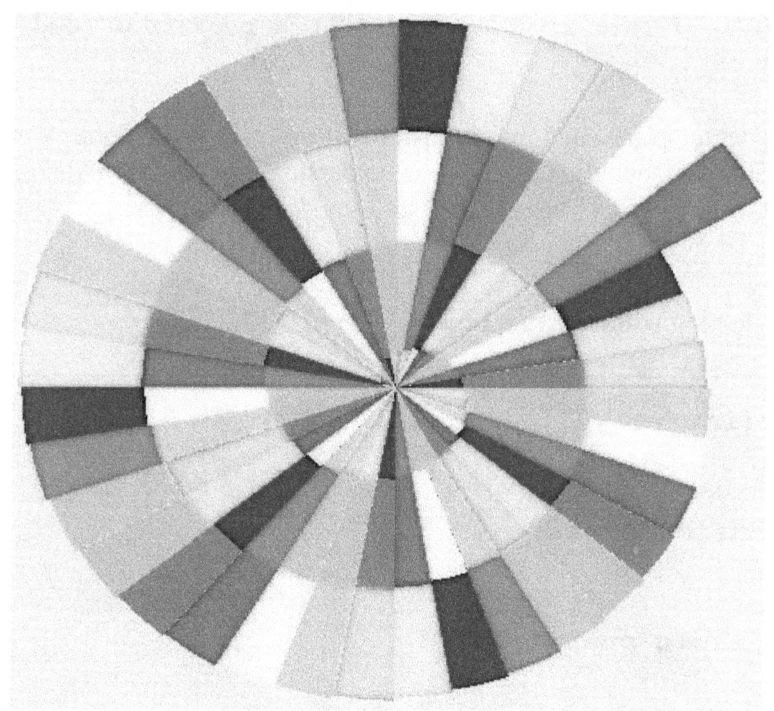

TEMPLATES FOR BASIC TIME PERFORMANCE COMPLEXITY CATEGORIES

Templates for each of the following basic complexity categories

$\Theta(\log n)$, $\Theta(n)$, $\Theta(n \log n)$, $\Theta(n^2)$, $\Theta(n^3)$, $\Theta(a^n)$, and $\Theta(n!)$

We conclude time efficiency analysis discussion by providing sets of templates for the following seven basic time performance complexity categories: log n, n, n log n, n^2, n^3, a^n, and n! which arise commonly in time analysis.

The complexity category of some function f(n) is the set of all functions that have the same asymptotic growth as f(n), which is denoted $\Theta(f(n))$. The template examples are simple, their time efficiency analysis is not mathematically intensive, and they correspond to various algorithms. If we replace basic operations with printing one letter, we can use such algorithms as representatives of the entire equivalence class of all performance equivalent algorithms.

In addition, we provide various template modifications that do not affect asymptotic growth. Modified templates remain in the same complexity category. Finally, we list several problems discussed in previous chapters for which algorithm time performance belongs to a given complexity category.

The approach of using templates and their transformations not only complements the introduction to time efficiency analysis, but also can improve understanding of this traditionally difficult topic since it uses a bottom up approach as opposed to a standard top-down.

1) Templates for logarithmic run time

```
void logRec(int n)                                    // Template 1
{
  if (n==1)
    do one basic operation
  else
  {
     do one basic operation
     logRec(n/2)
  }
}
```

Variations for template 1) that preserve logarithmic asymptotic time include one or more of the following:

- Base case can be when variable n has one or more of given initial nonnegative constant values.
- Performing one basic operation in the base case and/or recursive step can be replaced with performing any constant nonnegative number of basic operations.
- Recursive call can be made with variable n reduced by any positive constant factor b>=2

instead of reducing n by factor 2. This can be verified by applying Master theorem. If a=1 (only one recursive subproblem invoked) and nonrecursive cost is constant (which means d=0) then $a=b^d$, and for any b>=2 T(n) is logarithmic.

- The order of performing basic operations and invoking the recursive method may be interchanged without affecting the time performance.

The following simple algorithms with logarithmic time performance can be used to illustrate the template 1:

Determine the number of digits in binary representation of a given decimal number n.
Determine the number of digits of a given integer number n.
Convert base ten (decimal) number n into base 2 (or base 3, or 8, or any other positive constant)
Calculate a^n based on formula $a^n = 1$ if n=1, $a^n = (a^{n/2}) * (a^{n/2})$ if n>1, and n is even, and $a^n = a * (a^{n/2}) * (a^{n/2})$ otherwise.
For given integer number n return the string of digits representing number n in base 3.
Display the digits of a given positive integer n in reverse order.
For given list and given target perform binary search.
For given list and given target perform ternary search.

2) Templates for linear run time

```
void linearRec(int n)                                    // Template 2
{
  if n=1
     do one basic operation
  else
  {
     do one basic operation
     linearRec(n-1)
  }
}
```

Variations for template 2 include one or more of the following:

- Base case can be when variable n has one or more of given constant values, or in base case nothing is done and it is omitted.

- Performing one basic operation can be replaced with performing a constant number of basic operations in the base case or in the recursive step part.
- Recursive call can use variable n decreased by any positive constant c instead of n-1.
- Order of performing basic operations and invoking the recursive subproblem may be interchanged.

```
void linearRec2(int n)                                    // Template 3
{
  if n=1
     do one basic operation
  else
  {
     do one basic operation
     linearRec2(n/2)
     linearRec2(n/2)
  }
}
```

Variations for template 3 that preserve linear asymptotic time include one or more of the following:

- Base case can be when variable n has one or more given constant values, or in base case nothing is done and it is omitted,
- Performing one basic operation can be replaced with performing any constant number of basic operations in the base case or in the recursive step part,
- The order of performing one or more basic operations and making two recursive calls to sub-problems can be any permutation of those three steps,
- Several basic operations can be done before, in between, or after the two recursive calls.
- Instead of two recursive calls, each reducing size by two, k recursive calls, each reducing size by k can be invoked. This follows from Master theorem. If a=k, b=k, and d=0 implies $a>b^d$ since $k>k^0$. So, T(n) is in $\Theta(n)$.

The following simple algorithms with linear time performance can be used to illustrate the above discussed templates 3 and 4:

Template 2	Determine the sum of first n numbers.
Template 2	Determine the sum of first n squares.
Template 2	Determine the sum of first n cubes.
Template 2	Determine the sum of array elements.

Template 2	Determine the harmonic sum.
Template 2	Determine the largest array element.
Template 2	Determine the index of the largest array element.
Template 2	Perform a linear search for a given key in the array with n elements.
Template 2	Calculate a^n based on the formula $a^n = 1$ if n=1, $a^n = a * a^{n-1}$ for n>1.

Template 3	Calculate a^n based on the formula $a^n = 1$ if n=0, $a^n = (a^{n/2})*(a^{n/2})$ if n>0 and n even, and $a^n = a*(a^{n/2})*(a^{n/2})$ otherwise. Two identical recursive calls to sub-problems of size n/2 are made in the code. (Operator / is integer division.)
Template 3	Determine sum of all array elements by invoking two subproblems to determine sums of first and second half of the array elements.
Template 3	Determine sum of all array elements by invoking three subproblems to determine sums of first, second, and last third of the array elements.

3) Templates for n log n time

```
void n_log_n_Rec (int n)                                    // Template 4
{
  if n=1
     do one basic operation
  else
  {
     do n basic operations
     n_log_n_Rec (n/2)
     n_log_n_Rec (n/2)
  }
}
```

Variations for template 4 that do not affect asymptotic **n log n** time performance include one or more of the following:

- Base case can be when variable n has one or more given constant values, or in base case nothing is done and it is omitted.
- Any positive number of basic operations can be performed in the base case instead of just

one.

- During the recursive step the basic operation can be performed an+b times where a and b are positive integer constants.
- Basic operations can be performed before, after or in between the two recursive calls.
- Instead of two recursive calls with problem size reduced by factor two, we can call k recursive subproblems of size reduced by k. (According to Master theorem, if a=k, b=k and d=1, equality $a=b^d$ is always true.) Time performance remains n log n.

The following simple algorithms with *n log n* time performance can be used to illustrate template 4 and its variations:

Template 4	Draw letter "A" n log n times by invoking two recursive subproblems of size n/2.
Template 4	Apply merge sort to sort list of n items.
Template 4	Draw the squares using the following algorithm. Base case is when side length is less than or equal to a given constant. No basic operation is performed in that case. At the highest level of recursion, outline of a square centered at x,y with side length equal to n is drawn. Square's interior is not filled with color. In addition, four recursive calls are made with center coordinates shifted in each of the following four directions: 1) up, left, 2) up, right, 3) down, left, and 4) down, right. Each of the four recursive calls has size n reduced by factor 4. (Similar to example 6 in chapter 3, except that subproblems reduce size to n/4 instead of n/2.)

4) Templates for quadratic run time

```
 void quadraticRec(int n)                          // Template 5
{
   if n=1
      do one basic operation
   else
   {
      do n basic operations
      quadraticRec (n-1)
   }
 }
```

Variations to template 5 that preserve quadratic run time include:

- Base case can be when n equals 0, or any constant positive number instead of 1.

- In base case several basic operations may be performed instead of one.
- Recursive call to a sub-problem can be invoked with n decreased by any positive integer instead of 1.
- Nonrecursive cost can perform an+b basic operations instead of n. (Constant a can be positive integer and b can be any integer.)
- The order of invoking a recursive subproblem, and performing one, or more basic operations, can be interchanged.

```
void quadraticRec2(int n)                                    // Template 6
{
  if (n > 1)
  {
     do n basic operations
     quadraticRec2 (n/2)
     quadraticRec2 (n/2)
     quadraticRec2 (n/2)
     quadraticRec2 (n/2)
  }
}
```

Variations to template 6 that preserve quadratic run time include:

- Base case can be when n equals 0, or any constant positive number(s) instead of 1.
- In base case any constant number of basic operations may be performed instead of only one.
- Nonrecursive cost can perform a n + b basic operations instead of doing n basic operations. (Constant a can be any positive integer and b can be any integer.)
- The four recursive calls to sub-problems of size n/2, and performing n basic operations, can be done in any order.

The following simple algorithms with quadratic time performance can be used to illustrate the templates 5 and 6:

Template 5	Draw given letter "A" n^2 times. Invoke one recursive subproblem of size n-1.
Template 5	Perform selection sort for given list of n elements.
Template 5	Perform insertion sort for given list of n elements.
Template 5	Perform bubble sort for given list of n elements.
Template 6	Draw outlines of squares by invoking four recursive subproblems of size n/2 as shown in example 6 in chapter 3.

Template 6	Draw C-curve as done in example 5 in chapter 3.

5) Templates for cubic run time

```
void cubicRec(int n)                              // Template 7
{
  if n>1
  {
     do n² basic operations
     cubicRec(n-1)
  }
}
```

Variations to template 7 include

- Base case can be for n equal to a given constant or n less than given constant.
- Performing any constant number (including possibly none) of basic operations in base case.
- In recursive step, performing n^2 basic operation can be replaced by performing any quadratic function of n of basic operations.

```
void cubicRec2(int n)                             // Template 8
{
  if n>1
  {
     do one basic operation
     cubicRec2(n/2)
     cubicRec2(n/2)
     cubicRec2(n/2)
     cubicRec2(n/2)
     cubicRec2(n/2)
     cubicRec2(n/2)
     cubicRec2(n/2)
     cubicRec2(n/2)
  }
}
```

Variations to template 8 that preserve cubic time include

- Base case can be for n equal to a given nonnegative constant or n less than given positive constant, and we can perform any constant number of basic operations.
- In recursive step, performing one basic operation can be replaced by performing a constant number, a linear function of n, or a quadratic function of n of basic operations. (In Master

theorem a=8, b=2 and d equal to 0, 1, or 2 makes $a > b^d$ which results in cubic time.)

The following simple algorithms with cubic time performance can be used to illustrate the above discussed templates 5 and 6:

Template 5	Determine the largest element in a three dimensional array of size n x n x n.
Template 5	Print the letter "A" n^3 times by invoking one subproblem of size n-1.
Template 5	Determine if three given sets of cardinality n are disjoint.

Template 6	Draw squares filled with color so that at highest level we draw one square with side of length n and centered in the center of the window. In addition, call recursively eight subproblems each reducing n by factor two and being centered E, W, S, N, NE, NW, SE, and SW of the current center. Stop when n falls below the given threshold.
Template 6	Draw outline of squares so that at highest level we draw one square with side of length n and centered in the center of the window. In addition, call recursively eight subproblems each reducing n by factor two and being centered E, W, S, N, NE, NW, SE, and SW of the current center. Stop when n falls below the given threshold.
Template 6	Draw circles filled with color so that at highest level we draw one circle with radius equal to n and centered in the center of the window. In addition, call recursively eight subproblems each reducing n by factor two and being centered E, W, S, N, NE, NW, SE, and SW of the current center. Stop when n falls below the given threshold.

6) Templates for exponential run time

```
void expRec(int n)                                  // Template 9
{
  if n=1
     do one basic operation
  else
  {
     do one basic operation
     expRec (n-1)
     expRec (n-1)
  }
}
```

Variations to template 9 that preserve exponential time include:

- Base case can be for n equal to or less than a given constant instead of for n=1.
- Performing a constant number of basic operations at base case or anywhere during the recursive step.

```
void expRec2(int n)                                   // Template 10
{
  if n=1
     do one basic operation
  else
  {
     do one basic operation
     expRec2 (n-1)
     expRec2 (n-2)
  }
}
```

Variations to template 10 that preserve exponential time include:

- Base case can be at n equal to any nonnegative constant or less than a given positive constant instead of 1.
- Performing a constant number of basic operations at base case.
- Performing a constant number of basic operations anywhere during the recursive step.

```
void expRec3(int n)                                   // Template 11
{
  if n=1
     do one basic operation
  else
  {
     expRec3 (n-1)
     do 2^n basic operations
  }
}
```

- Variations to template 11 that preserve exponential time include
- Base case can be for n equal to or less than any given positive constant instead of for n=1.
- Performing a constant number of basic operations at base case instead of just one.

The following algorithms with exponential time performance can be used to illustrate the templates 9, 10, and 11:

Template 9	Tower of Hanoi

Template 10	Find n-th Fibonacci number

Template 11	Print letter "A" 2^n times by invoking one recursive subproblem of size n-1.
Template 11	Determine all subsets of the set {1,2, . . .,n}.

7) Template for n! run time

```
void factorialTimeRec(int n)                    // Template 12
{
  if n=1
     do one basic operation
  else
  {
     for( int i=1; i<=n; i++)
       factorialTimeRec (n-1)
  }
}
```

Variations to this template that preserve n! running time include:

- Base case can be for n equal to a given nonegative constant or n less than given positive constant and possibly performing constant number of basic operations instead of performing one.
- Recursive step may have loop body that invokes recursive subproblem of size n-1 and performs constant number of basic operations.

The following algorithms with n! time performance can be used to illustrate the template 12:

Template 12	Print all permutations for given n by using HeapPermute algorithm
Template 12	Print letter "A" n! times.

LITERATURE

[Aho74] Aho, A.V., Hopcroft, J.E., Ullman, J.D. *The Design and Analysis of Computer Algorithms.* Addison-Wesley, 1974.

[Aho83] Aho, A.V., Hopcroft, J.E., Ullman, J.D. *Data Structures and Algorithms*. Addison-Wesley, 1983.

[Aho95] Aho, A.V., Ullman, J.D. Foundations of Computer Science. C Edition. Computer Science Press, 1995.

[Car04] Carrano, F. M., Prichard, J. J. *Data Abstraction and Problem Solving with Java:* Walls and Mirrors. Updated ed. Person-Addison Wesley, 2004.

[Col92] Collins, W. J. *Data Structures: An Object Oriented Approach*. Addison-Wesley, 1992.

[Cor90] Cormen, T.H., Leiserson, C.E., Rivest, R.L., Stein, C. *Introduction to Algorithms*. 2nd ed. MIT Press, 2007

[Das08] Dasgupta, S., Papadimitriu C., Vazirani U. Algorithms. Mc Graw Hill, 2008.

[Goo02] Goodrich, M.T., Tamassia, R. *Algorithm Design: Foundations, Analysis, and Internet Examples.* John Wiley & Sons, Inc. 2002.

[Goo06] Goodrich, M.T., Tamassia, R. *Data Structures and Algorithms in Java.* 4th ed. John Wiley & Sons, Inc. 2006.

[Knu76] Knuth, D. E. Big omicron, big omega, and big theta. *ACM SIGACT News, volume* 8, 1976. pp 18-24.

[Knu97] Knuth, D. E. *The Art of Computer Programming. Vol 1: Fundamental Algorithms*, 3rd ed. Addison-Wesley, 1997.

[Knu98] Knuth, D. E. *The Art of Computer Programming. Vol 2: Sorting and Searching*, 2nd ed. Addison-Wesley, 1998.

[Kof94] Koffman, M. *Software Design Data Structures in Turbo Pascal*. Addison Wesley, 1994.

[Kru87] Kruse, *Data Structures and Program Design*. Prentice Hall, Inc. 2nd ed. 1987.

[Nap95] Naps, Nan, *Introduction to Computer Science Programming, Problem Solving and Data Structures.* 3rd ed. West Publishing Company. 1995.

[Nea04] Neapolitan, R., Naimipour, K. *Foundations of Algorithms Using Java Pseudocode*. Jones and Bartlett Publishers. 2004.

[Pev05] Pevac, I. *Recursive Examples in Java*. XanEdu-OriginalWorks. 2005.

[Pev16] Pevac, I. *Practicing Recursion in Java.* CreateSpace. 2016.

[Sha98] Shaffer, C. A. A Practical Introduction to Data Structures and Algorithm Analysis. Java Edition. Prentice Hall. 1988.

[Sed03] Sedgewick, R. *Algorithms in Java*. Parts 1-4. 3rd ed. Addison Wesley, 2003.

[Sed04] Sedgewick, R. *Algorithms in Java*. Part 5. 3rd ed. Addison Wesley, 2004.

[Sed11] Sedgewick, R. Wayne, K. *Algorithms*. 4th ed. Addison Wesley, 2011.

[Ste90] Stevens, R. T. *Fractal Programming in Turbo Pascal*. M&T Books. 1990.

ABOUT THE AUTHOR

Irena Pevac is a professor of computer science at Central Connecticut State University. She has over twenty years of experience teaching Algorithms in undergraduate and graduate level courses. Other computer science courses that she taught are: introductory programming courses, data structures, database, artificial intelligence, theory of computation, and theoretical computer science.

She published four books and over 40 papers in journals and conference proceedings. The domain of her research publications includes automata and formal languages, computability, artificial intelligence, theorem proving, database design, algorithm time performance, and teaching.

www.ingramcontent.com/pod-product-compliance
Lightning Source LLC
Chambersburg PA
CBHW060453060326
40689CB00020B/4514
9781539088868